NEW ENGLAND WOMEN OF SUBSTANCE

NEW ENGLAND WOMEN OF SUBSTANCE

*Fifteen Who
Made a Difference*

J. NORTH CONWAY

COVERED BRIDGE PRESS
NORTH ATTLEBORO, MASSACHUSETTS

"What do women want?" —*Sigmund Freud*

Copyright © 1996 by J. North Conway. All rights reserved. No part of this book may be reproduced by any means, except brief quotations in a review, without the written permission of the publisher.

ISBN 0-924771-81-X

10 9 8 7 6 5 4 3 2

Covered Bridge Press
North Attleboro MA

NEW ENGLAND WOMEN OF SUBSTANCE

CONTENTS

Acknowledgements		vii
Introduction	A PLACE BY THE RIVER	1
Chapter 1	FAITH OF OUR MOTHERS Elizabeth Pole	7
Chapter 2	THE FIRST LADY OF THE AMERICAN REVOLUTION Mercy Otis Warren	16
Chapter 3	SOLDIER GIRL Deborah Sampson	26
Chapter 4	THE MOTHER OF THANKSGIVING Sarah Hale	33
Chapter 5	CRAZY IN AMERICA Dorothea Dix	44
Chapter 6	KINDERGARTEN CULTURE Elizabeth Peabody	57

CONTENTS

Chapter 7	THE LITTLE WOMAN WHO MADE A BIG WAR Harriet Beecher Stowe	64
Chapter 8	FIELD OF THE HEAVENS Maria Mitchell	75
Chapter 9	ANGEL OF THE BATTLEFIELDS Clara Barton	83
Chapter 10	THE WITCH OF WALL STREET Hetty Green	95
Chapter 11	MOTHER OF INVENTIONS Margaret Knight	104
Chapter 12	KEEPER OF THE LIGHT Ida Lewis	110
Chapter 13	PURPLE MOUNTAINS' MAJESTY Annie Peck	117
Chapter 14	MEASURE FOR MEASURE Fannie Farmer	123
Chapter 15	A SELF-DETERMINED LIFE Blanche Ames	131
Epilogue	BRIDGET SMILING	139
About the author		144

ACKNOWLEDGEMENTS

This book is dedicated to Ava and Nora Sullivan, Casey White, Jessie Ratcliffe, and Emily Floyd—all part of a whole new generation of American women.

The world, as well as we have left it for you, is yours. Good for you. Do the best you can, have fun, good luck, and don't forget to shut off the lights before you leave.

I could not have done this book without the help of Ruth Sullivan at Bristol Community College.

I would also like to thank *Cape Cod Life* magazine for publishing my article on Maria Mitchell; the *Taunton Daily Gazette* for publishing articles about some of the women in this book; fellow New England authors and friends, Scott Ridley and Michael Tougias, and my agent, Alison Picard.

Also, many thanks to the staff of the Taunton Public Library and the Taunton Old Colony Historical Society for their help.

Special thanks are extended to my good and dear friend, and avid reader, Joyce Longo; Bettina Briggs, who has been a constant source of encouragement during the writing of this book; Stacy Cushner; The Reverend David Keyes; and Walden Radio's Rob Mitchell, who has given voice to many grateful New England authors like myself.

Thank you one and all!

INTRODUCTION
A Place by the River

This book is about fifteen New England women, who, although obscured by time, made significant contributions to our culture and society, often despite great odds.

There are, of course, far more than just fifteen women from New England who made a difference. I subjectively chose the women who appear in this book, based on my own interest in them. I found them to be fascinating human beings who made some very extraordinary accomplishments. I hope you find them equally fascinating.

The original title of this book was *Ladies Choice: Fifteen New England Women Who Made a Difference.*

I chose the original title from the very old practice that used to occur at dances when women were given the opportunity to choose their own partner for a dance. In the square dance of American History, I felt the fifteen women in this book made some very significant and defining choices.

By and by, you will be reading all about these women and their accomplishments, but before you begin, I want to tell you a little bit about how I came to write this book.

2 INTRODUCTION

Whenever I am introduced to people, the first question I am usually asked is, "How did you become a writer?" I will tell you.

I became a writer because a very long time ago, someone told me that being a writer was the best job in the world. I was told that if you were a writer you could travel all over the world, and as long as you were near a mailbox, you could mail off your stories to publishers and make a living.

To an impressionable child, that sounded pretty good—travel all over the world and just be close to a mailbox. So I decided that I would become a writer.

Let me tell you what happened. I only managed to get half of the instructions right. I became a writer, but I never left my home town of Taunton, Massachusetts. I have lived here all my life.

I grew up in a small section of Taunton by the Taunton River known as "The Brickyard." It was named that because the Stiles and Hart Brick Company was located there.

The men and women who lived in this neighborhood and worked at the brickyard turned out thousands of bricks each day that were shipped down river on barges to faraway places.

I grew up in a house that faced the river and the brickyard, and spent many evenings sitting on my porch watching the brickmen come and go up the street.

The Stiles and Hart Brickyard has long since closed and the old neighborhood where I grew up is filled with condominiums and fast food joints.

I now live in an old Victorian house at another place by the Taunton River. I have lived in this old house most of my adult life. I have not traveled far. But, I can readily assure you, there is a mailbox right up the street.

Most nights, in the spring, summer, and fall, I still sit out on my front porch, facing the river, and watch the world go by. Sometimes friends and neighbors stop by.

Bruce White and Jeff Mansfield, who live in houses nearby, often join me on my porch on hot summer nights, where we sit and talk, smoking cigarettes and drinking blue margaritas late into the evening.

Blue margaritas are a specialty of mine. They are made of tequila, lime juice, blue curacao and crushed ice.

Jeff, a high school teacher, who neither drinks or smokes, for reasons I will not go into now, is one of the city's premier amateur golf players, having won just about every golf tournament in the city.

One hot summer night, while we were out on my porch, he gave me a few tips on how to improve my golf game. Later that evening, once the blue margaritas did their work, I took it upon myself to drive a golf ball off my front porch with a nine iron. Luckily, it safely flew over the roof of the three-story, historic Victorian home across the street and plopped into the river. Good for me.

Bruce, a salesman of sorts, who is not adverse to either smoking or drinking, said, "Nice shot, Jack," seeing that I had not careened the ball into any stained glass windows next door.

People I know all call me "Jack." The only people who don't call me Jack are people I grew up with in The Brickyard, and, of course, my family—my dear sisters Judy and Betty, and my mother, who all call me "Jackie."

I, of course, forgive them, endlessly, for calling me Jackie, loudly, in the middle of crowded malls or at other places where throngs of people gather.

I was once invited to speak at a local Rotary Club function. A well-established Taunton attorney, Theodore Stronjy, a man with whom I grew up in The Brickyard, introduced me to the audience as "Jackie Conway."

I, of course, returned the favor, and thanked my good, and dear friend, "Teddie Stronjy."

It was shortly after "Jackie's Infamous Golf Ball Incident," that I decided I should begin work on this book.

Idle hands are the devil's workshop, especially when swinging a golf club, not to mention the effects of too many blue margaritas.

I decided to write about these women because for my entire life I have been fortunate to have been surrounded by women who have made a significant difference in my life. Among them, my mother, Irma, who still steadfastly remains living in the old Brickyard section of Taunton, despite all its changes, and who has been a constant source of inspiration to me; my lovely wife Julia, who has given me more love and joy than anyone truly deserves; my sisters, Betty and Judy—despite the fact that they still call me "Jackie"—my mother-in-law, Mary; Aunt Lee; sisters-in-law Chrissy, Martha, Lisa and Ruth; and most recently, my lovely daughter-in-law, Leah.

For my entire life, I have been surrounded by a multitude of unique, interesting and inspiring women.

Another reason I wrote this book is that I grew up and have lived all my life in the only city in America that historians claim was founded by a woman—Elizabeth Pole.

The Wampanoag Indians called Taunton "Cohannet," which means "a place by the river."

For centuries, the Taunton River, stretching 44 miles from its beginning in Bridgewater, Massachusetts, to its mouth in Mount Hope Bay in Fall River, has been a vital source of commerce, industry and entertainment.

The City of Taunton and its river is rich in lore and history. It is the third longest river in Massachusetts; the first successful iron works was started along a tributary of the Taunton River in 1656; the Baylies Iron Works along the river forged the anchor for the U.S.S. Constitution ("Old Ironsides"); the first four- and seven-masted schooners were built at shipyards along the Taunton River; the first schooner with an engine was built along the river; and the first legalized lottery in Massachusetts was held in Taunton to raise money to dredge the river. That's only the half of it.

Elizabeth Pole reportedly bought this tract of land from the Wampanoag Indians in 1639 for a bag of beans, a jackknife and a cow. And there were no closing costs.

She also founded the first church in the community, First Parish Church, which is a stone's throw (depending upon whether you use a nine iron or not) from where I live. It is now a Unitarian Church. It is the church I belong to and walk to every Sunday. The mailbox, of which I previously spoke, is directly across the street from this church.

Elizabeth Pole was a leader in the Taunton community, dabbling in politics, religion, business and commerce. Robert Treat Paine, a signer of the Declaration of Independence, wrote the inscription on the monument erected to her after her death in 1654, and the city fathers placed her likeness on the official seal of the city. Good for her.

I have read many books and articles about her and I can tell you this, from a historical perspective, Elizabeth Pole was a real pistol. That is not authentic historical jargon, but it will suffice. A real pistol.

Some historians have tried to debunk the story of Elizabeth Pole founding the City of Taunton. I do not know why, other than that most of these debunkers are men.

I only have one bit of advice for them—save your breath. The story about Elizabeth Pole may be mythical, I admit, but it is a darn good story. Her story lends beauty, hope and inspiration to our collective lives.

As my dear friend and fellow Taunton author, Scott Ridley, says, "Myths put mountains in our collective horizon." He's right. We could all stand a few more mountains in our collective horizons, I think.

Let me tell you about another Taunton woman who made a difference—Salome Lincoln. In 1829 Salome Lincoln led what some historians have called the first labor strike in America. On April 29, 1829, she led nearly 100 women off their jobs in the Taunton knitting mills to protest a proposed cut in wages by the mill owners.

The ladies rallied on the Taunton green to protest what they considered unfair labor practices. Nothing like it had ever been seen by Tauntonians, or anyone else for that matter—100 women, marching silently, solemnly, resolutely through the city streets to protest management's treatment.

As the instigator of the strike, Lincoln was fired by the mill owners, but they dropped the pay cut and in fact, based on newspaper clippings of the day, they marginally increased wages for the women garment workers. Salome Lincoln left Taunton shortly after the strike and moved out West, where she became one of the first female preachers.

This book is filled with stories about New England women, like Elizabeth Pole and Salome Lincoln, who made choices in their lives that ultimately had a dramatic effect on all our lives. Some of them I am sure you have heard of before. Others might not be as well known to you. Certainly, all of them are unique figures in the cultural development of New England and our country.

I believe their stories are important, not only because of what they did and the contributions they made in our past, but because they can serve as an inspiration for all women today to do the things that need to be done, and the choices that have to be made, in the future. Thank you.

1 FAITH OF OUR MOTHERS
Elizabeth Pole, 1589–1654

"There are many ways in which we can honor the memory of Elizabeth Pole: in our language, our leadership, our example, our theology, our worship."

PEOPLE, PLACES AND EVENTS: The first child born in the American colonies was a female. Virginia Dare was born in 1587 on the Roanoke Island colony off the coast of North Carolina.

She disappeared three years later, part of the ill-fated Roanoke Lost Colony, carried off, it is presumed, by Crotan Indians, along with the 116 other inhabitants of this early American settlement. Other brave women colonists soon followed.

In 1602, Captain Bartholomew Gosnold became the first Englishman to land in New England, at what is now New Bedford, Massachusetts. He later explored the New England coast and was responsible for naming both Cape Cod and the island of Martha's Vineyard.

The first permanent English colony was established in Jamestown, Virginia, in 1607.

By 1630, the entire population of new world settlers was six thousand people. In 1639, the population had grown to nearly thirty thousand. The native American population at the time was approximately one million.

The first settlers of the Massachusetts Bay Colony landed at Salem Harbor in 1629. They were led by John Winthrop, who later became the first Governor of Massachusetts.

Winthrop was instrumental in founding Boston's first Puritan Congregationalist church.

In 1637, Winthrop banished Anne Hutchinson from the colony, charging her with heresy. She fled to nearby Rhode Island.

During this period, the first public Thanksgiving Day was celebrated. It was designated as a day of fasting.

In Dorchester, Massachusetts, the first public school supported entirely by taxes was established in 1639, while in Cambridge, Massachusetts, Harvard College was established.

In 1643, the first American textile mill was built in Rowley, Massachusetts, and the first successful ironworks was founded along the banks of the Saugus River, near Lynn. It was founded by former Massachusetts Governor John Winthrop.

During the same period, Elizabeth Pole is credited with being the first woman in America to found a successful ironworks company, in Taunton, Massachusetts.

* * * * *

Although she was born in England, Elizabeth Pole's roots are firmly planted in New England history and lore.

She was, based on many historical accounts, the first woman to found a settlement in America, the first to establish a church, and the first in New England to engage in manufacturing.

I have taken the title of this chapter from a sermon delivered at the First Parish Unitarian Church in Taunton in May,

1989, by The Reverend David Keyes. I was at the time and remain a member of this church, which Elizabeth Pole founded in 1639.

The Reverend Keyes was and remains a dear friend, although now a distant one since his departure to California. The purpose of his sermon was to defend Miss Pole against the rising tide of criticism aimed at debunking her role as the first woman founder of a community in America. Good for him.

"Male historians seem intent on unseating Elizabeth Pole as the leader of the settlers of Taunton and the first congregation of this church. These men, I am afraid, do not take her very seriously," The Reverend Keyes said.

There is very little historical information available about Miss Pole; many of Taunton's historical documents about her were lost in a devastating fire in 1838 that gutted much of the city. Her life story has been pieced together from historical fragments, stories and myths. Still, it is quite clear that Elizabeth Pole was the driving force in all the endeavors of this small, industrial city in southeastern Massachusetts.

For those who doubted her role in the development of the community and her place among the first women to do so, The Reverend Keyes had this to say, "It needs to be understood that history itself is not an exact science. It is more a matter of selecting the most likely fiction from a selection of possible fictions, of piecing together a story from scraps of a jigsaw puzzle when you know full well that several of the key pieces are permanently missing."

Now, after the extensive and grueling research I have undertaken to piece together this chapter on Elizabeth Pole, I feel compelled to add my own comments on the subject. The "history" of Elizabeth Pole, pieced together from those available fragments, is a wonderful and inspiring story—part myth, perhaps. But no more a myth than the history of

General George Washington crossing the Delaware at Valley Forge in the middle of a raging blizzard, standing up heroically in the bow of a small boat. Are we to believe that General Washington actually did this? Or is it what we would like to believe, and in doing so, provide generations of Americans with an inspiring and noble image?

To truly understand the enormous and far-reaching contributions made by women like Elizabeth Pole and other New England women, you must first understand that their struggle was twofold—against both Church and State. Both these institutions taught that silence and obedience were female virtues. When a woman chose to speak up for her rights, she was called "unwomanly." Elizabeth Pole was compelled to leave her comfortable life in Taunton, England, for religious as well as economical and political reasons.

At the time of her journey to the New World, the Church was more than happy to reaffirm, and still somewhat continues to reaffirm, the simple-minded doctrine of Saint Paul, who wrote, "Wives, submit yourself to your husbands as to the Lord. The head of every man is Christ and the head of every woman is the man.

"Let the women learn in silence and all subjection. But I suffer not a woman to teach nor to usurp authority over the man, but to be in silence."

The earliest New England government's attitude toward women could be best summed up in the words of the Massachusetts Bay Colony's first governor, John Winthrop, who admonished Anne Hutchinson, one of New England's earliest and most infamous religious radicals, with the words, "We do not mean to discourse with one of your sex."

Hutchinson was tried, convicted and banished from Massachusetts into the Rhode Island frontier by Winthrop and the Puritan clergy for the outrageous act of holding prayer meetings at her home and for knowing the Scriptures better than many of her male counterparts.

Elizabeth Pole was also banished to the wilderness, but not by either the Church or the State. It was of her own choosing that she left the Plymouth Bay Colony and settled in southeastern Massachusetts, because of her desire to worship as she believed and to conduct herself with each and every freedom afforded to men in the New World.

Elizabeth Pole was the third oldest child of Sir William and Lady Mary Pole of Taunton, England. Her grandfather was a personal friend of Queen Elizabeth and her successor, King James.

Elizabeth could have lived out her life in ease and comfort on her father's large estate in England if she desired. But instead, she came to America, to find her fortune and worship as she pleased.

She made two trips to America, the first in 1635. Her first trip was a scouting mission to the Plymouth Bay Colony to examine the prospects for establishing a free religious settlement in the New World. When she decided it could be done, she returned to England to secure the provisions she would need.

Given the hardships and dangers faced in crossing the Atlantic, the feat of crossing the ocean twice was itself remarkable.

As a young woman of wealth and leisure in England, Elizabeth was not interested in cultivating feminine social graces as her sisters were content to do. Instead, she preferred working outdoors with the estate's laborers and devoted much of her time to religious thought and reading.

Her father, who was a noted scholar, had little time to oversee the upbringing of Elizabeth or any of his other daughters. This he left in the hands of his wife. When Mary Pole died, Elizabeth, who was still a teenager, took control of managing her father's large estate. She oversaw all the farming, gardening and livestock operations.

She grew up in a period of great religious turmoil in England. The old Church beliefs were being challenged by radical clergymen who wanted to purify the church and return to the teachings of Jesus Christ.

Many of her countrymen and women fled to America in search of religious freedom.

As early as 1632, Elizabeth met and became inspired by the ideas of The Reverend William Hooke, a radical Anglican priest. Hooke, like many religious revolutionaries, wished to break from the teachings of the Church of England.

His radical ideas on the freedom of religious worship inspired Elizabeth.

She and Hooke were joined in their radical religious discussions by another religious dissenter, The Reverend Nicholas Street.

Their discussions led to only one conclusion: in order to worship as they pleased and throw off the yoke of the oppressive Church of England, they too would have to flee to America.

It was during this same period that Elizabeth invested heavily in a company promoting fishing and trade in New England. When the company failed and she lost her investment, her desire to regain her lost fortune, along with her religious beliefs, compelled her to journey to America.

She traveled to the Plymouth Bay Colony with her younger brother William. On their first mission they discovered a world, although not perfectly suited for what they hoped to accomplish, at least vast enough to explore and settle themselves.

They returned to England where Elizabeth secured the provisions she needed—home furnishings, farm tools and livestock—and returned to Plymouth. This time, she brought with her The Reverend William Hooke and his family.

The entourage stayed in Plymouth for only a short period of time. She discovered quickly that the religious and social freedoms she had come to find in America were not to be found in the strict confines of the Puritan community.

Puritan women in Plymouth were treated like only so much livestock—their worth diminished, their ideas dismissed. They were expected to bear and raise children, tend to cooking and housework and do many of the outdoor chores. The men were busy attending religious meetings and overseeing the workings of the government.

Knowing that much of the land south of the colony had yet to be explored and settled, she and her brother set out on foot to find a tract of fertile land for their own settlement.

They carried most of their provisions on their backs and marched some thirty-five miles through rough, unexplored territory—swamps and overgrown underbrush. Finally they came to a Wampanoag Indian settlement called "Cohannet." The land along either side of the river, now named the Taunton River, was lush, rich and perfect for farming.

Elizabeth negotiated with Massasoit, the chief of the Wampanoags, for the purchase of the land. She traded the Wampanoags corn, beans and a jackknife for a large tract, and in 1639 became the owner of an estate twice the size of her father's in England. She also became the first woman in America to settle a town.

Land was cleared and simple homes were built. She laid out farms and established fishing sites. One of her first priorities was to establish a church—the Church of God—on the site where the First Parish Unitarian Church now stands. William Hooke became the church's first minister.

Along with the settlement and the church, she established the first ironworks along the banks of the Taunton

River, making her the first woman in America to engage in manufacturing.

Along the banks of the river she established a furnace and hired men familiar with iron production. The swamps and ledges of the Taunton community were rich with iron ore which could be mined and processed. From this humble beginning she began an industry that grew throughout southeastern Massachusetts.

Naming Taunton after her home in England, Elizabeth Pole lived and prospered there for the next fifteen years, overseeing or being consulted on much of the town's development.

When she died in 1654 at the age of sixty-five, she left a will in which she bequeathed one cow to sustain the church she had established. The cow was to be selected by the Deacons of the church, also executors of her will.

According to The Reverend Keyes, although a cow may seem like an odd gift by today's standards, "... it should be remembered that in the settlement of the frontier, cattle were better than gold. And although it is difficult to calculate an exact exchange rate, it is probably safe to say that a cow was worth thousands of dollars."

William Pole, Elizabeth's younger brother, who had first come to America with his daring sister, later became a deputy to the Plymouth Court. In his position, he advocated the right of women to think and act for themselves, just as his sister had done.

Now, more than 350 years after her death, Elizabeth Pole is remembered and honored as the founder and leader of the Taunton community. Her likeness appears on the city's official seal.

Robert Treat Paine, a signer of the Declaration of Independence and a member of the church Elizabeth Pole first established in Taunton, wrote the inscription on the stone monument erected over her gravesite.

"Here rests the remains of Miss Elizabeth Pole, a native of Old England, of good Family, Friends and Prospects.

All of which she left in the Prime of her life, to enjoy the Religion of her Conscience, in this distant Wilderness.

A great Proprietor in the township of Taunton; a Chief Promoter of its Settlement and its incorporation, 1639–40.

About which time she settled near this spot,
And having employed the opportunity of her
Virgin state
In Piety, Liberality
And sanctity of manners."

The Reverend David Keyes ended his sermon in 1989 by noting that everyone could honor the memory of Elizabeth Pole, and in doing so, honor the memory of all New England woman who made a difference, "in our language, our leadership, our example, our theology, our worship." In closing, he asked the entire congregation to "honor all women, and those who have nurtured us," by making a long overdue change in the closing hymn, by singing, "Faith of Our Mothers." Elizabeth Pole, I think, would have approved.

Suggested Reading

Adams, James. *The Founding of New England* (1921).
Dexter, E. A. *Colonial Women of Affairs* (1924).
Golemba, Beverly E. *Lesser-Known Women* (1964).
Hosmer, J. K. *The History of New England* (1908).
James, Edward T., ed. *Notable American Women 1607–1950* (1971).

2 THE FIRST LADY OF THE AMERICAN REVOLUTION
Mercy Otis Warren, 1728–1814

"Whose energies and abilities were executed by the use of her pen on all occasions and in various shapes in promoting the principles that resulted in the Independence of America."

PEOPLE, PLACES AND EVENTS: In 1776, Abigail Adams wrote to her husband, John, imploring him to "remember the ladies and be more generous and favorable to them than your ancestors."

John Adams, who was in Philadelphia helping to frame the Declaration of Independence, and who would later become the country's second President, paid no attention to his wife's request. Most of the freedoms and rights American patriots fought for would elude women for another 150 years, when they were finally given the right to vote.

In April 1775, the first battle of the American Revolution was fought in Lexington, Massachusetts, when patriot militiamen attacked British troops marching to nearby Concord to seize military supplies and provisions hidden there. The war lasted eight years, 1775–1783.

In 1787, delegates to the Constitutional Convention wrote the U.S. Constitution. A year after that it was ratified by nine of the thirteen new American states. The other four states ratified the document later.

As powerful and far-reaching as the Constitution was, it did not enjoy popular support. Those opposed to it feared the document lacked the basic guarantees for individual freedoms of worship, speech, assembly and freedom of the press.

Supporters of the Constitution reluctantly promised that if the document was ratified, it would be amended to include these guarantees.

In 1791, the Bill of Rights, the first ten amendments to the Constitution, was adopted.

In 1789, George Washington was elected as the country's first President. In 1796, John Adams succeeded him. In 1800, Adams was defeated in his reelection bid by Thomas Jefferson.

The population of the country was approximately three million.

* * * * *

With her pen, Mercy Otis Warren drove one British Governor out of the colonies, drove America's second President from office, and helped ensure every Americans' individual civil rights by advocating the Bill of Rights.

Born in Barnstable, Massachusetts, in 1728, she was a poet, dramatist, patriot and historian during the great upheaval in American history, earning her the title of "The first lady of the American Revolution." Historians have called her "perhaps the most remarkable woman who lived during the Revolutionary period."

Her endeavors were by no means typical, but neither was her upbringing and education. She wrote scathing and oftentimes bawdy commentaries, not only about the British rule in America, but about Americans she felt had betrayed the ideals of the American Revolution, among them the country's second president, John Adams.

She was the third child and first daughter of thirteen children born to James and Mary Otis. She grew up on a large and prosperous farm on rural Cape Cod, where her father served as a judge and worked as a lawyer and farmer.

Although all the Otis sons were educated and prepared for college, none of the daughters was given a formal education. Because of her inquisitive nature and obvious intellect, Mercy was allowed to sit in on her older brother James' lessons. Like James, she was tutored by her uncle, The Reverend Jonathan Russell, a local minister, and was given free reign of his extensive library. She was a voracious reader, especially in the areas of history and literature.

Mercy and James were the intellectual stars of the family, and James often tutored his younger sister in politics and world events. Because of their father's position in the community, the two children were often exposed to political debates, focusing primarily, because of her father's political leanings, on patriotism in the colonies, rather than on loyalty to the British crown.

When her brother was admitted at fourteen to Harvard College, Mercy was heart-broken to lose a good and trusted friend, as well as an intellectual equal. While her brother was gone, she busied herself with her domestic education, learning, as all young colonial women did, to cook, sew and tend to a household.

Her brother stayed in constant contact with her during his years away, writing to her almost every day and passing along to her the wealth of knowledge and political thought he had come in contact with at Harvard. Through his intellect and abilities as an orator, James became a student leader at the college.

When he graduated in 1743, Mercy made her first trip from Cape Cod to Cambridge to attend the ceremony. There she was introduced to many of her brother's classmates, among them James Warren of nearby Plymouth, and John Adams, who was destined to become the country's second president following the Revolution.

James later opened a law practice in Plymouth, where he continued his friendship with James Warren, now a successful merchant in the town. Mercy and James Warren's acquaintance blossomed into romance.

In 1754, when she was twenty-six years old, she and James Warren were married. They moved into his family estate in Plymouth, where their household soon became a hotbed of political and literary debate. Mercy engaged in both. Like her brother James, she was passionate and unyielding about the politics of revolution.

As the conflict with the British government grew more intense, Mercy became more politically active. Not content merely to listen to the arguments about American independence, she turned her talents toward writing about it.

At the time, her father was a Justice of the Peace, her husband a member of the Massachusetts Legislature, and her brother a lawyer for the British government.

Taking her lead from her brother, Mercy soon found herself attacking British rule.

In protest of the British law allowing customs agents arbitrarily to enter any home or business to search for and seize illegal contraband (goods not taxed by the British), James Otis resigned his position as a lawyer for the government and became an outspoken revolutionary leader.

James was adamantly opposed to the British rule governing search and seizure within the colonies, and he argued his case against the British law before the Massachusetts Supreme Court. It was during his argument, which lasted more than four hours, that he coined the now famous phrase, "Taxation without representation is tyranny!"

His words soon became the rallying cry of the coming American Revolution.

"Then and there, the child of Independence was born," John Adams said of James Otis's speech.

James rose quickly in the ranks of the leaders of the American Revolutionary movement. As he rose, his younger sister Mercy tried to keep pace. Unable to express herself in courtrooms or public forums like her brother, she turned to writing poetry and plays that advocated the revolutionary cause.

When she wrote and published "The Squabble of the Sea Nymphs," a poem celebrating the Boston Tea Party (December 16, 1773), she quickly became the American Revolution's literary star.

Her first play, "The Adulateur," was published anonymously in 1772 in two installments in the *Massachusetts Spy*, a Boston-based newspaper. It portrayed the British-appointed Governor of Massachusetts, Thomas Hutchinson, as an ardent foe of those who loved liberty.

Within a year she published "The Defeat," a play depicting Hutchinson as a turncoat who would shift his loyalties from the British to the patriot cause without provocation.

Shortly after its publication, the ridiculed Hutchinson was dismissed as Governor and sent home to England in disgrace.

After Hutchinson's removal as Governor, the British sent General Thomas Gage to serve as the Governor of the rebellious commonwealth.

Not about to let Gage off the hook, in 1775 Mercy published another play, "The Group," in which she predicted that Gage would attack the town of Concord, Massachusetts, where much of the rebel supplies were being stored. Her prediction turned out to be correct.

Following the outbreak of the Revolution, her husband was named paymaster general by General George Washington.

After General Gage's British forces were driven from Boston in March 1776 and the war moved south, Mercy continued to write, letting her farm in Plymouth fall into disarray in her husband's absence.

Although the Revolutionary forces marched south to engage the British, her husband was asked to stay behind and organize the first American Navy to combat the British on the seas. It was a relief to her to have him stay behind, and out of harm's way, but he seldom had time to visit with her in Plymouth to care for the farm or help with the upbringing of their five sons.

Her brother James, a firebrand during the early stages of the Revolution, was forced to spend his remaining days at his family's Barnstable farm, recovering from wounds inflicted by an irate British customs agent.

In 1769, James was attacked and bludgeoned by the customs officer during an argument in a Boston tavern. He never fully recovered from the severe beating, and was forced to leave the Revolution to his many followers.

Mercy was devastated by the attack on her brother.

"I wish to know every circumstance of this guilty affair. Is it possible that we have men among us, under the guise of the officers of the Crown, who have become assassins?" she wrote.

Despite her brother's condition and her husband's absence, she continued to write.

In 1776 she wrote "The Blockheads: or The Affrighted Officer, a Farce, 1776." In it she depicted General Gage as a cowardly tyrant.

But her sharp-edged political pen was not limited to attacks on the British forces. After the British evacuated Boston, the city began to prosper, and many of its more elite inhabitants resumed their lives of luxury. Mercy wrote "The Motley Assemblage," a play that ridiculed that elite, who began to spend lavishly on luxuries after the British retreated. She scorned them for carrying on in such a way, while soldiers were dying elsewhere in the cause of liberty.

For Mercy, the tragedy of the Revolution was not just limited to abstract ideals about liberty and government. Just before the war ended, one of her five sons, Winslow, who was serving in the American Navy, was captured by the British and sent to prison. Her son James, Jr., also serving in the Revolutionary cause, was wounded and his leg amputated. And her son, Charles, who was attending Harvard College at the time, developed tuberculosis and died.

In 1783, her beloved brother James succumbed to the wounds he had suffered fourteen years previously. A year after his death, her father died.

She, herself, was stricken with smallpox and spent a year in bed recovering. Through all her own personal tragedies, sickness and the war, she persevered, continuing to write scathing commentaries about the British rule.

In 1790, she published a collection of poetry and two plays, "The Ladies of Castille," and "The Sack of Rome." Both plays were filled with patriotic spirit, full of romance, women and high drama. Her reading audience loved them both.

"It is certain that in The Ladies of Castille, the sex will find a new occasion of triumph," Alexander Hamilton wrote in 1791 about her play.

Her major work, begun in 1775, was *History of the Rise, Progress and Termination of the American Revolution, Interspersed with Biographical and Moral Observations.*

The book took her more than twenty-five years to complete, and comprised three volumes. Finally published in 1805, it brought to a head her relationship with John Adams.

In the work, she accused Adams of betraying "the principles of the American Revolution," and charged him with being "guilty of talents and much ambition."

Her split with Adams was based on the existing division within the Federalist Party after the war.

Adams demanded a government strong enough to squelch any subsequent rebellion in the new America. The anti-Federalists, to which Mercy belonged, wanted to protect the individual civil liberties of the colonists, maintaining that those liberties were what the war had been fought for.

Following the publication of her massive work, and although Adams had been among one of the first to encourage her to write it, he complained publicly that "History is not the province of the Ladies."

With Adam's election as the second American President (1797–1801), and the Federalists in control of the new American government, Mercy and her family fell into disrepute.

Her husband was overlooked for a position within Adams' administration, despite his many contributions to the Revolutionary cause. And one of her remaining sons, George, now a practicing lawyer, was blacklisted during the Adams presidency.

But the battle between Adams and Mercy was not over. She actively and publicly opposed the signing of the U.S. Constitution because she felt the new Constitution did not provide any guarantees of individual rights for American citizens.

In a long article called, "Observations on the New Constitution and on the Federal and State Conventions," she wrote of her objections to the Constitution.

Despite being shunned by Adams and the Federalist Party, she maintained a large and influential reading public.

Publication of her article contributed to the passage of the first ten amendments to the U.S. Constitution, called the Bill of Rights, one of America's foremost documents securing individual rights.

Adams was never able to escape Mercy's wrath.

"His prejudices and his passions were sometimes too strong for his sagacity and judgment," she wrote about the country's second President.

During his administration, he passed the Alien and Sedition Acts, designed to oust French subversives from the country and close down all anti-Federalist free presses. Both bills were violations of the individual liberties that Mercy and others fought so hard to maintain.

Both Mercy and her husband worked against the reelection of Adams in his second term and he was defeated, replaced by Thomas Jefferson, whose political thinking was more closely aligned with Mercy.

"I pray to present my homage of my great respect to Mrs. Warren. I have long possessed evidence of her high station in the ranks of genius" Jefferson wrote to her.

In 1808 her husband James, a neglected and much maligned founder of the American Revolution, passed away. Adams, a former Harvard classmate and friend during the earliest days of the Revolution, refused to offer his sympathies to Mercy.

When war with Britain again threatened in 1812, she joined her old foe, John Adams, in opposition to it. She even convinced the town of Plymouth to send to Congress a proclamation declaring that the town refused to fight in such a war. Her efforts went unheeded.

In the last months of her life, at the age of eighty-six, she fought her last battle, this one literary rather than political.

In August 1814, two months before her death, another writer claimed credit for writing the inspiring patriotic play, "The Group," which originally appeared in 1775. Ironically it was her old nemesis, John Adams, who came to her defense. Adams verified that the play was written by Mercy.

In proclaiming her authorship of "The Group," he wrote that Mercy Otis Warren was a woman, "Whose energies and abilities were executed by the use of her pen on all occasions and in various shapes in promoting the principles that resulted in the Independence of America."

She continued to write until the day of her death. She died on October 19, 1814, at the age of eighty-six, in Plymouth, Massachusetts, where she had spent most of her life, and was buried at Burial Hill in Plymouth.

Suggested Reading

Anticaglia, Elizabeth. *Twelve American Women* (1975).
Anthony, Katherine. *First Lady of the Revolution: The Life of Mercy Otis Warren* (1958).
McHenry, Robert, ed. *Liberty's Women* (1980).
Raven, Susan, and Alison Weir. *Women of Achievement* (1981).
Smith, William. *History as Argument: Three Patriot Historians of the American Revolution* (1966).

3 SOLDIER GIRL
Deborah Sampson, 1760–1827

"Fleet as a gazelle, bounding through swamps many rods ahead of her companions."

PEOPLE, PLACES AND EVENTS: In 1775, the Continental Congress appointed George Washington as the Commander in Chief of the Continental Army.

In 1776, General Washington captured 1,000 mercenary troops in the Battle of Trenton, New Jersey, and a week later his troops won the Battle of Princeton.

At the Battle of Saratoga, New York, the Continental Army defeated British forces and captured 6,000 troops.

These early victories heartened the Revolutionary forces, but a series of losses left Washington's army in disarray—cold, hungry and poorly armed.

In 1781 both British and Revolutionary armies suffered heavy losses during the Battle of Guilford Court House in North Carolina.

The military phase of the American Revolution ended in 1781, when British General Cornwallis surrendered at Yorktown, Virginia. Cornwallis and his 8,000 troops had only occupied Yorktown for three months before the surrender.

The war did not officially end until the Treaty of Paris was signed by the British in 1783.

After the war, Washington was elected the country's first President. In 1796, he delivered his farewell speech to Congress. He died three years later.

In 1800, Washington, D.C., became the official capital of the country, succeeding Philadelphia. The first President inaugurated there was Thomas Jefferson in 1801.

The population of the country had grown to five million people. The most populated state was Virginia, and the largest city was Philadelphia. There were nearly one million slaves reported in the country. Massachusetts was the only state in the country not to have slaves.

*****

Deborah Sampson was the only woman to fight shoulder to shoulder in the military ranks during the American Revolution. Disguised as a boy, she enlisted in the Continental Army and for two years served in battle as a gallant soldier.

According to historical accounts, she served courageously and was "fleet as a gazelle, bounding through swamps many rods ahead of her companions."

She was born in Plympton, Massachusetts, in 1760, the oldest of six children. Her father, Jonathan Sampson, was a farmer, and her mother, Deborah (Bradford) Sampson, was a descendant of Massachusetts Governor William Bradford.

Deborah grew up in dire poverty. When her father's farm failed, Jonathan Sampson abandoned his family and went to sea to find his fortune.

It was difficult for Mrs. Sampson to bring up her large family, so she was forced to make her children work as servants at other successful farms in the region.

When she was ten years old, young Deborah went to work as a servant in the home of Jeremiah Thomas in Middleboro, Massachusetts. She worked there for eight years. Working on the Thomas farm as part of the household staff, she developed into a strong, skilled, and capable young woman.

She attended the Middleboro public school for only a short period of time and was otherwise taught by the Thomas family. Although she had a limited education, it was enough to allow her to become a teacher for a short period after her service with the Thomas family ended.

But she was not content with life as a school teacher. She was a tall, strong, plain-looking woman, and although she had not traveled much beyond the bounds of the small Middleboro farming community, she had a lust for adventure.

With nothing further to bind her to either the Thomas family or the town, and filled with the romantic notion of seeing the country, she walked from Middleboro to Boston and from there out to the western part of the state to Bellingham, where she enlisted in the Continental army using the name Robert Shurtleff.

With her hair cut short and wearing men's britches and waistcoat, she entered the army undetected. Despite her high cheekbones, smooth unshaven skin and noticeably high-pitched voice, no one suspected her. Many of the young men who enlisted in the army were young boys, so her feminine qualities were not questioned.

She joined the 4th Massachusetts Regiment under the command of Captain George Webb. Like many of the young recruits, she was forced to endure long marches through hostile territory, but her stamina and her adaptability to the circumstances helped her to conceal her identity from both her commanding officers and her fellow soldiers.

Webb's forces engaged in a series of small skirmishes, in which Deborah performed her duties admirably.

According to General Henry Knox, commander of the Continental forces at West Point, she served as a "faithful and gallant soldier and at the same time preserved the virtue and chastity of her sex unsuspected and unblemished."

During the battle of Tarrytown, New York, she received a saber wound to her leg, but refused to allow doctors to treat her, fearing her sex would be discovered. Instead, she cared for the wound herself and resumed her duties.

During a skirmish with British forces a few weeks later at East Chester, she received a far more serious wound when a musket ball shattered part of her already wounded leg. Still she refused medical attention.

Despite her wounds, Deborah marched with her regiment from New York to Philadelphia. On route, she became sick and delirious with a fever and had to be hospitalized. It was not until she was finally admitted to a Philadelphia hospital that her gender was discovered.

Although shocked by the discovery, her commanding officers, most notably General Knox himself, were not shaken to find that one Robert Shurtleff, who had served so gallantly in engagements throughout the last year of the war, was indeed a woman. General Knox awarded her an honorable discharge after she recovered from her fever and gave her a modest sum of money.

She returned to her native Massachusetts in November 1783 where she went to live with an uncle in Sharon, Massachusetts. Back home, she let her hair grow out and began dressing as a woman again.

After the war, she met and married a Sharon farmer, Benjamin Gannett, in 1785. She and her husband had three children, Earl, Mary and Patience. Although reports of her adventures during the war began to attract notice, not all of it was good. In her former hometown of Middleboro, the First Baptist Church, where she had been a member, excommunicated her for "dressing in men's clothes, and enlisting as a soldier in the army," and claimed that she had "for some time before behaved very loose and unChristian like."

With three children to raise and her husband's farm failing, she attempted to earn a living by writing the story of her adventures. In 1797, she sold her biography to Massachusetts publisher Herman Mann, who published her biography under the title, *The Female Review.*

This romanticized version of her story included Deborah having a Middleboro suitor that she was trying to elude as the reason why she disguised herself and enlisted in the army. In another part of the book a beautiful girl in Baltimore fell in love with her, not knowing her true identity, and Deborah also had to elude her.

Along with the publication of the book, she began a lecture series, beginning with an appearance at the Federal Street Theater in Boston in 1802. She traveled throughout Massachusetts and New York, expounding on her romanticized escapades as the first woman to fight as a soldier during the Revolutionary War.

Neither the lecture series or the book provided her with enough money to live on. She decided to appeal to Congress for a pension. In 1792, she received a stipend from the Massachusetts legislature of approximately $34 a year.

In 1804, she sought help from one of the Revolutionary War's most renowned heroes, Paul Revere (1735–1818), who lived in nearby Canton, Massachusetts. By the time she sought Revere's help she was forty-four years old. Revere was so taken with her and her plight, he wrote to Congress on her behalf.

"Humanity and Justice obliges me to say, that every person with whom I have conversed about Her, and it is not a few, speak of her as a woman of handsome talents, good morals, a dutiful wife, and an affectionate parent," Revere wrote.

"She has told me that she has no doubt that her ill health is in consequence of her being exposed when she did a soldier's duty and that while in the army she was wounded.

"When I heard of her spoken of as a soldier, I formed the idea of a tall, masculine female, who had a small share of understanding, without education and one of the meanest of her sex. When I saw her and discoursed with her I was agreeably surprised to find a small effeminate woman, whose education entitled her to a better situation in life.

"I have no doubt your humanity will prompt you to do all in your power to get her some relief."

In March, 1805, she was placed on the pension list of the government at a rate of four dollars per month. The amount was later substantially increased.

Despite being the first woman to receive a government pension for her military duty, her financial difficulties continued. She wrote constantly to her advocate Paul Revere asking him for help.

In 1806, she wrote,"I blush at the thought that after receiving ninety and nine good turns as it were, my circumstances require that I should ask the hundredth—the favor that I ask is the loan of ten dollars for a short time." Revere, who had already proclaimed her "handsome talents," readily lent her the money.

Life in Sharon was hard and relentless, but as in all things she had endeavored to do, Deborah Sampson persevered.

After her death in 1827, her husband, Benjamin, petitioned the federal government for a pension for himself. His argument to Congress was that for many years he had paid steep medical bills for his wife, and that her illness was due to her military service to the Revolutionary cause.

In 1838, nearly a dozen years following his petition to Congress, the federal government approved the pension. An "Act for the relief of the heirs of Deborah (Sampson) Gannett, a soldier of the Revolution, deceased," was approved and a payment of approximately $500 per year was awarded to the remaining heirs of Deborah Sampson.

Benjamin Sampson died before the pension was awarded, so the money went directly to their children.

Deborah Sampson, America's first woman soldier, died in 1827, at the age of sixty-six, and was buried in the Rockridge Cemetery in Sharon, Massachusetts.

Suggested Reading

Bach, Shirley J. *Women and the Military* (1977).
Birdwell, Russell. *Women in Battle Dress* (1942).
Fraser, Antonia. *The Warrior Queens* (1989).
Salmonson, Jessica Amanda. *The Encyclopedia of Amazons* (1991).
Tinling, Marion. *Women Remembered* (1986).
Wertheimer, Barbara Mayer. *We Were There* (1977).

4 THE MOTHER OF THANKSGIVING
Sarah Hale, 1788–1879

"Whoever thought I could make so much money doing something as pleasant as writing."

PEOPLE, PLACES AND EVENTS: The necessity to earn a living compelled many women into literary endeavors, and New England was a hotbed of literary enterprises by women.

One of the first was Anne Royal, born near Baltimore, Maryland (1769–1859). She was fifty years old when she began publishing her travel journals. Nearly penniless, she traveled the country writing about social issues of the times, including education, prison reform, childhood education and labor.

She finally settled in Washington, D.C., where she began publishing a four-page weekly newspaper called *Paul Pry*. The publication included the country's first gossip columns, devoted to covering the exploits of Washington's elite, including President John Adams.

The publication evolved into *The Huntress*, in which she exposed graft and corruption within the government, and attacked public officials. As a result, she became known as the "Grandmother of Muckrakers," and was the country's first gossip columnist.

Another prominent New England woman publisher was Lydia Francis Child (1802–1880), who was only twenty-two years old when she published *Hobomok: A Tale of Early Times*, the first exposé of the daily workings of Puritan life in Massachusetts. Born in Medford, Massachusetts, she later published *The Frugal Housewife*, a feminine version of Benjamin Franklin's *Poor Richard's Almanac*.

Among these female literary leaders was Sarah Hale of New Hampshire. It was through her literary efforts that Thanksgiving Day was proclaimed an official United States holiday.

The first publicly celebrated Thanksgiving Day was held in February 1631 in the Massachusetts Bay Colony. Rather than a day of feasting, it was designated as a day of fasting.

It was first celebrated as a national holiday on November 26, 1789, when President George Washington proclaimed the date as a day to celebrate the U.S. Constitution.

In 1863, President Abraham Lincoln declared Thanksgiving as an official national holiday. He designated the last Thursday in November as the date, and it was observed on this date for more than seventy-five years.

In 1939, President Franklin Roosevelt moved the holiday forward to help the country's failing economy by promoting earlier Christmas shopping.

In 1941, Congress adopted a resolution making the last Thursday of November the official holiday date.

*****

Sarah Hale of Newport, New Hampshire, appealed to five U. S. Presidents in her bid to have Thanksgiving declared a national holiday. As America's first woman editor, she wielded unique power, but it still took her nearly 30 years to see her dream come true.

In 1863, following the bloody Civil War battle at Gettysburg, her pleas finally reached a receptive audience in President Abraham Lincoln. He wholeheartedly agreed with her contention that all of the country needed a day to "lay aside our enmities and strifes on this one day."

Lincoln's aim was to solidify the Union states into a single day of peace and thanksgiving.

"Not in celebration of military victory but in gratitude for a year filled with the blessings of fruitful fields and healthful skies," his proclamation read.

After three long years of bloody fighting, the war-weary country embraced the chance to stop the bloodshed, even if for one day, and give thanks for the bounty the nation offered up to them.

President Lincoln declared Thanksgiving Day an official national holiday on Oct. 3, 1863, designating the last Thursday in November as the official holiday. It was held on this date for more than 75 years.

As the editor of the largest and most popular magazine in the country, *Godey's Lady's Book,* Sarah Hale held a powerful and influential position within American culture and society.

Each year she devoted a special edition of the magazine to Thanksgiving and Thanksgiving menus. Her articles and editorials were instrumental in teaching Americans how to celebrate the holiday correctly.

One of her magazine editorials proclaimed that declaring Thanksgiving as a national holiday would be "a grand spectacle of moral power and human happiness."

Household advice columns in the magazine covered everything from how to stuff a turkey to making pumpkin pies.

She was joined in her campaign by other popular magazines of the day. Pen and ink drawings of supposed "Old-Fashioned Thanksgiving Day," filled the pages of the November issues of magazines across the country.

During the pre-Civil War Era, there were many people throughout the country who felt that a holiday like Thanksgiving could be a useful tool in the effort to preserve the Union. At the time many Southern States were on the verge of succession.

Hale felt that a national holiday that all Americans celebrated to count their blessings, would encourage national unity. Her sentiments were not shared by everyone. By 1850 most governors had proclaimed Thanksgiving as a state holiday, but not the state of Virginia.

Hale wrote to Governors across the country urging their support for the holiday, and most, North and South, were receptive. But not Governor Henry H. Wise of Virginia.

"I am aware that Virginia has not often joined in keeping this festival but this year (1850) when as I trust the Democratic Party will gain a victory as will ensure the perpetuity of our beloved Union, surely the Old Dominion will gladly keep the day of Thanksgiving," Hale wrote to Wise.

"This theatrical national claptrap of thanks has aided other causes in setting thousands of pulpits to preaching Christian politics instead of humbly letting the carnal kingdom alone," Wise wrote back. By "other causes," Wise meant the abolition movement. Wise had long been a slave-owner and states rights advocate.

But, it is not only for being the tireless promoter of Thanksgiving that Sarah Hale is remembered.

Along with being the first women editor in the country, she was the author of the book that Harriet Beecher Stowe's *Uncle Tom's Cabin* was modeled after, the founder of the Boston Seaman's Aid Society to help the families of merchant sailors, the driving force behind the completion of the Bunker Hill Revolutionary War Monument, the author of one of the country's most well-known children's poems, and an innovator in American publishing.

Added to all this, she was a staunch supporter of education for women and was instrumental in helping to establish Vassar College in New York, one of the first all-woman colleges.

The tiny mill town of Newport, New Hampshire, still celebrates Sarah Hale's memory and perseverance with a plaque on the town common, a special reading room set aside in the local library, and a literary medal given every year to a noteworthy New England writer.

She was born in Newport, New Hampshire, in 1788. In 1813, at the age of twenty-five, she married David Hale, a lawyer. Before marrying she had worked for seven years as a schoolteacher.

While her husband's law practice thrived, she tended to her four children: David Emerson, Horatio, Frances Ann and Sarah Josepha.

In 1822, her husband got pneumonia and died. Two weeks after his death, she gave birth to her fifth child, William George.

She was left as young widow with five children to support, during a period in the country when there were few opportunities for women to earn a decent living.

"I don't mind poverty for myself. Nothing can add to my grief, and nothing could take from it. But I do not want our children to be deprived of the things necessary for a happy, healthy life. And an education," she said.

In order to make ends meet, she opened a millinery shop in her home, but she had little talent for it and the business failed.

In 1823, at the urging of a family friend, she turned to writing.

"I would rather write, but I cannot earn a living for myself and family that way," she protested at first. How very wrong she was.

Within the year, Jacob Moore, a Concord, New Hampshire, publisher, published her first book of verse, *The Genius of Oblivion and Other Original Poems*, written by "A Lady of New Hampshire." The tiny book sold enough to inspire her to write a novel.

In 1827, Boston publisher Bowles and Dearborn published *Northwoods: A New England Tale*. The novel promoted the notion that life in the north was superior, based on its democratic bent and religious virtues. She contrasted this environment with what she perceived as the decadent, slave-holding Southern society.

In the novel, she devoted a full chapter to the description of what a typical New England Thanksgiving Day might be like. Her opinion, stated in the novel, was that Thanksgiving "should be the same as the Fourth of July, a national holiday."

The book was a tremendous success. No one had ever written a novel daring to deal with the differences between the societies of the North and South. And, it was the first book to address the issue of slavery. It caused a sensation throughout the country and was reprinted in England, France and Germany.

"Whoever thought I could make so much money doing something as pleasant as writing?" she said.

The success of the novel led in 1828 to a job as editor of the Boston-based *Ladies' Magazine*. It was one of the earliest magazines devoted exclusively to women, and the first edited by a woman. She moved her family to Boston to take the job.

The first edition of the magazine was a mere 52 pages, printed on small, 8 x 4 inch sheets. She wrote all the copy for the first issue herself, often using assumed names to conceal her identity.

Scouring the first printed issue, she found a number of typographical errors in the copy and demanded to correct them all by hand on each of the 1,000 issues printed. The first issue of *Ladies' Magazine* edited by Hale was distributed with all her handwritten corrections. It was still a great success.

"You have produced a revolutionary book," John Putnam, the publisher of the magazine, told her. Hale was not so sure.

Each succeeding issue attracted more subscribers.

She spoke out in favor of infant education (kindergartens) and demanded that girls should receive an education equal to boys. She urged that women should be trained as teachers of young children and introduced an ongoing fiction series within the pages of the magazine, inviting American authors to submit material.

She was one of the first to publish a young unknown poet, Edgar Allen Poe, in the pages of her magazine.

Among her many innovations was to print bylines with stories and articles, encouraging authors to sign their names to their work. "When an author signs his name, it has the effect of vouching for the truth of what he writes," she maintained. Previously, many authors used only their initials or *nom de plumes*, just as she had when she published her first book of poetry.

Along with her editing duties at the magazine, she continued to write poetry. As a gift to her five young children, she published a collection of poetry she had written for them. In 1830 she published *Poems for Our Children*, which included one of the world's best-known child's verse, "Mary

Had a Little Lamb." This book was also an immediate success.

Dr. Lowell Mason, a prominent Boston composer, set her poems to music. His intent was to promote the teaching of music and singing in public schools. In 1831, Mason finished his book, *The Juvenile Lyre*. The songbook was given to school children in Boston and was the first book used to teach children to sing as part of their classroom studies.

Not long after the publication of the children's book, she became active in several patriotic and humanitarian causes.

On an excursion with her children to view the famous Bunker Hill Monument, she was saddened to discover that the monument was not finished. She took it upon herself, using the pages of her magazine, to organize women to raise funds to finish the monument. Her pleas for fund-raising donations were so successful that, in 1842, the Bunker Hill Monument was at last completed.

There is a plaque on the monument that simply states, "Bunker Hill Monument, started by men in 1825 and finished by the ladies in 1842."

Another cause that attracted her attention was the plight of the families of Boston seamen. She was appalled at the poverty, filth and hunger she discovered along the "shantytowns," where the families of Boston sailors lived.

Boston seamen, she maintained, were the backbone of Boston's prosperity. Their voyages were long, often two years at a stretch, and difficult. While they were gone, their wives and children had to exist as well as they could, often living in slum conditions without proper food or medical care.

Hale wrote extensively about their plight and offered a solution—an organization dedicated to helping the poor families of seamen. She held a rally where hundreds of the city's most prominent citizens turned out. Entering the rally, Hale was loudly applauded.

"I am simply a Boston woman interested in improving a shameful situation," she told the throngs. The result of the rally and the editorials led to the founding of the Boston Seaman's Aid Society to help the families of merchant sailors.

In 1837 *Ladies' Magazine* merged with *Lady's Book*, a popular women's magazine published in Philadelphia by Louis A. Godey. Hale was asked to remain as the editor of the new *Lady's Book and Magazine,* which later became simply known as *Godey's Lady's Book*. In 1841 she moved her family and her editorial offices to Philadelphia.

Godey's Lady's Book became the most influential and widely distributed women's magazine of its time. In 1860, the national circulation of the magazine was approximately 150,000.

The magazine influenced everything from fashion to home design throughout the country. When *Godey's* advocated a new bonnet style for women, manufacturers wasted little time copying the fashion. When it promoted designs for model American homes, carpenters and builders found themselves building homes like the ones in *Lady's Book*.

But Godey had competition. George Graham, another Philadelphia publisher, launched a new magazine, *Graham's Gentleman's Magazine*. He hired a new editor, Edgar Allen Poe. Poe's work helped increase *Gentleman's Magazine* circulation from a paltry 6,000 subscribers to approximately 40,000 and rising.

Godey and Hale did everything in their power to increase circulation and become the leading American magazine. But nothing seemed to work.

In the midst of this battle between the two giants of the magazine world, Hale came up with a revolutionary idea in magazine publishing, one that would ultimately seal the fate of Graham's magazine and Poe.

For years magazines had been publishing fashion plates and describing the latest fashions in dresses, coats, capes, bonnets and other outerwear. But no magazine ever dared breathe a word about undergarments.

Hale decided to begin describing women's underwear in *Godey's*. There would be no pictures, only articles describing what she referred to as "dainty, but sensible undergarments." She knew that neither Graham or Poe would dare to follow suit.

There was only one problem—she needed the right word for it. Underwear was too crude a phrase for the pages of her magazine and the word of the times, "unmentionables," was not descriptive enough. After reading a French journal, she settled on the French word *lingerie*.

"Good taste demands that a lady's lingerie shall be as dainty, yet simple as her purse permits," she wrote in the first edition featuring an article on women's underwear.

The edition caused an uproar. Letters poured into the magazine both praising and condemning her for the bold step. But more importantly, subscriptions increased, and *Godey's Lady's Book* roared pass *Gentlemen's Magazine*.

Ultimately, the word "lingerie" was incorporated into the lexicon of American publishing and language.

Sarah Hale retired as editor of *Godey's Lady's Book* in 1877 at the age of eighty-nine.

In her last editorial, written for the December 1877 issue, she wrote, "And now, having reached my 90th year, I must bid farewell to my countrywomen, with the hope that this work of half a century may be blessed to the furtherance of their happiness and usefulness in their divinely appointed spheres." She died in Philadelphia on April 30, 1879.

Suggested Reading

Burt, Olive. *First Woman Editor, Sarah Hale* (1960).
Finley, Ruth. *The Lady of Godey's* (1931).
Fryatt, Norma. *Sarah Josepha Hale: The Life and Times* (1975).
Parrington, Vernon. *Main Currents in American Thought,* vol. 2 (1927).
Trent, William. *The Cambridge History of American Literature* (1933).

5 CRAZY IN AMERICA
Dorothea Dix, 1802–1887

"I think even lying in my bed I can still do something."

PEOPLE, PLACES AND EVENTS: The years leading up to the Civil War produced a multitude of women social reformers. Among them was Elizabeth Blackwell (1821–1910), who was the first woman in the United States to receive a medical degree and the first female doctor of medicine. In 1853 she helped found the New York Infirmary and College for Women, the first such facility run entirely by women.

Mary Walker (1832–1919) was a nurse and later a physician who was appointed one of the first field surgeons during the Civil War. There were many more, including Dorothea Dix, who changed forever the way the mentally ill in this country were treated and cared for.

In the early days of America, women were the caregivers. They nursed the sick and infirmed; cared for the children and elderly and did their best to comfort and care for those less fortunate in body and mind.

Following the Industrial Revolution in the late 1700s, many women left their homes to go to work, leaving the caregiving to public institutions.

Cities and towns began to set up workhouses for the indigent, while others built jails, prisons and hospitals to care for those who could not care for themselves. Oftentimes, however, adequate and humane care was not provided.

Debtors and vagrants languished in prisons or jails. Children huddled in orphanages or workhouses. And the sick, especially those with mental illness, were banished to the deepest recesses of prisons and hospitals.

Their plight became the crusade of people like Dorothea Dix.

* * * * *

They say that most artists are mad, and that writers and poets are the maddest of all. If that is true, then every writer and poet in the country owes a debt of gratitude to Dorothea Dix, who forever changed the treatment of madness.

For nearly fifty years, despite her own debilitating physical illness, she relentlessly crusaded for the proper care of the mentally ill. She spearheaded the first prison and mental institution reforms in the country, and singlehandedly brought to public scrutiny the deplorable conditions in prisons and asylums.

She was responsible for the creation of more than thirty mental hospitals in America, as well as several in Japan and Europe. It was because of her tireless crusade that hiding those with mental illness was replaced with more sympathetic treatment and therapeutic care.

Dorothea Dix was born in 1802 in Hampden, Maine. Her father Joseph was a religious fanatic and an alcoholic. He had married Mary Bigelow, a Maine farm woman, who was eighteen years older than he was.

Joseph was a drifter who left his family for long periods of time to preach the gospel. He was drunk most of the time, and her mother was bedridden with numerous unexplained ailments.

"I never knew any childhood," she said when speaking about her early life in Maine.

This unhappy early life drove her to live with her grandparents in Boston when she was just ten years old.

Much of Dorothea's relentless spirit was a legacy from her grandfather, Dr. Elijah Dix, a wealthy Boston physician known for his tyrannical behavior and aggressiveness. Dr. Dix had been born into a poor family, but through sheer will and hard work, put himself through medical school and became wealthy through shrewd investing.

Her grandmother, Dorothy, was a proper New England lady, with a puritanical sense of duty and obligation. It was her grandmother who saw to it that Dorothea was properly educated and cared for.

Her grandmother was strict and unemotional, but she cared for Dorothea when her parents couldn't.

Her grandmother tried to instill in the young Dorothea perseverance and discipline, but the young girl often rebelled. Finally, her grandmother found the young girl too headstrong and sent her to live with her sister in Worcester, Massachusetts.

At fourteen, Dorothea realized that the only way to gain true independence was to attain some form of financial security. She began by opening a school of her own in Worcester.

In order to make herself appear older than she was, she often wore long dark dresses and tied her hair back in a severe hair style. Although she was attractive—tall and shapely, with dark blue eyes and dark curly hair—she disguised her good looks with somber clothes and a rigid demeanor.

One of her former students described her as "tall for her age, easily blushing, at once beautiful and imposing in manner, but inexorably strict in discipline."

She returned to Boston a year later to open a school for young girls on her grandparent's estate. At the same time she opened another school for poor children in the vacant rooms over the stable on the estate.

Running two schools, hardly finding time to rest, and in between time educating herself, all finally took its toll and she became seriously ill with a lung infection. She became so weak she could hardly speak and the pain in her lungs became so intense that she often walked around stooped from the pain.

During this period, she became acquainted with Dr. William Ellery Channing, a noted Boston Unitarian minister.

When Dorothea finally collapsed from sheer exhaustion and was unable to continue teaching at the two schools she had founded, Dr. Channing asked her to become the tutor for his own children. She left the city and spent the spring and summer at Channing's home in Rhode Island. She later traveled with the Channings to St. Croix, where she appeared to recover her health.

She returned to Boston and reopened her schools, but lasted only five years. She finally collapsed completely and was advised by her doctors to give up teaching and go abroad to rest and recuperate. She was just thirty-three years old.

In 1836 she traveled to England to rest and recover her strength. But she was not about to accept the life of an invalid as prescribed by her doctors in Boston.

She stayed in Liverpool with William Rathbone and his family, friends of Dr. Channing. While there, William Rathbone, a wealthy and prominent humanitarian, taught her about the horrors of the slums, child labor, prison conditions and the inhumane treatment of the insane.

She returned to Boston in 1838, still suffering from her lung condition.

At thirty-nine, she became somewhat resolved to living the life of a spinster, getting by on her inheritance and tending to her illness. But, in 1841 she was asked by a family friend if she would be interested in teaching Sunday School to a group of female inmates at the East Cambridge Jail. This was the turning point in her life.

In the basement of the jail she found four prisoners, all classified as mentally deranged. Their cell was unheated and dark and there was no ventilation. When she asked the jailkeeper why there was no heat in the cell, he told her that the insane could not feel the temperature.

She emerged from the jail with a new and overwhelming mission. She first went to court to demand that a stove be installed in the jail.

Dorothea suspected that the horrendous conditions at the East Cambridge Jail were not an isolated incident, so she set out to investigate the treatment of the insane in Massachusetts.

After the stove was installed at the East Cambridge Jail, she sought advice from Dr. Channing and other prominent reformers, including educator Horace Mann and Dr. Samuel Howe, president of the Perkins School for the Blind.

She was told that before the Massachusetts State Legislature would allocate funds to refurbish old institutions or build new ones, a detailed report on the conditions of the prison system would have to be made. Without any financial backing and on her own, Dorothea undertook the project.

For the next two years she traveled throughout the state, conducting a complete investigation of the condition of the insane in jails and prisons. What she uncovered was horrifying.

At the time, there were only a handful of hospitals in the country that provided humane and therapeutic care for the mentally ill. The overall attitude regarding those with mental illness was that they were depraved and needed to be confined and hidden from public view.

It was widely believed that evil had overcome the goodness of a person's soul in those with mental illness. The medical treatment of these poor souls called for them to be locked in cages, restrained with chains and left in the cold, dark recesses of state prisons and hospitals to starve.

In 1843, armed with incontrovertible evidence based on her research, she went before the Massachusetts legislature and presented her case. Her catalogue of horror and abuse was presented to the legislature as a memorial, calling attention to "the present state of Insane Persons confined within this Commonwealth, in cages, closets, cellars, stalls, pens! Chained, naked, beaten with rods and lashed into obedience!"

"I shall be obliged to speak with great plainness and to reveal many things revolting to the taste, and from which my woman's nature shrinks with peculiar sensitiveness," she told the legislature.

"But truth is the highest consideration. I tell what I have seen, painful and shocking as the details often are, that from them you may feel more deeply the imperative obligation which lies upon you to prevent the possibility of a repetition or continuance of such outrages upon humanity."

She presented hundreds of shocking examples, ranging from an old woman chained to a toilet, to a woman so filthy that Dorothea was unable to get near her because of the repulsive odor.

She ended her report with a plea for the legislature to provide enough funds and provisions to care for the mentally ill in a more humane and medically sound way.

Her report aroused public opinion. Massachusetts' reputation as an enlightened state was tarnished. Newspapers accused her of being an hysterical woman. Jailkeepers called her a liar. Many in the legislature called her report sensationalist.

Still, with the support of Channing, Mann and others, she persevered. A full-scale investigation was initiated by the legislature. When it found Dorothea's report to be accurate, the legislature passed a resolution calling for provisions to care for one hundred new patients at the state mental institution in Worcester. It was her first victory in a crusade to reform the care and treatment of mental illness.

She studied the current theories on insanity and interviewed physicians and teachers, expanding her knowledge on the subject. She traveled to Providence, Rhode Island to study the conditions there and then to New Jersey. The more she investigated, the more she determined that the inhumane treatment of the mentally ill was widespread and not just limited to Massachusetts. Her work became national in purpose and scope.

In each state she followed the same procedure, starting first with a detailed investigation of the current system and ending with a presentation of her independent research before the governing legislature. She seldom appeared or spoke in public. Her gentle demeanor and quiet dignity managed to keep hostility toward her at a minimum.

In Rhode Island she enlisted the support of Cyrus Butler, a wealthy and influential leader in Providence. Through her efforts Butler Hospital in Providence was enlarged to support more mentally ill patients.

In New Jersey in 1845 she helped pass a bill establishing a state mental hospital. A similar bill was passed by the legislature in Pennsylvania for a state-run facility in Trenton. She referred to the Trenton, New Jersey, hospital as her "first-born child," and it always held a special place in her heart. In later years, when she became too old and sick to travel anymore, she retired to the Trenton hospital to be cared for. In 1887 she died there.

Although enormously successful in her crusade, she felt at odds with her role. Many considered her work unfeminine.

"I am naturally timid and diffident, like all my sex," she wrote.

During the first four years of her crusade, she traveled 30,000 miles to more than eight hundred institutions that cared for the mentally ill throughout the country, and delivered stirring "memorials" before countless legislative bodies.

She became so well-known that travel companies gave her free passes on railroads and steamships as she moved from one end of the country to the other to deliver her message. Travel was difficult, subject to accidents, exposure and great discomfort, but she endured it all.

"I have travelled more than ten thousand miles in the last three years. I have visited eighteen state penitentiaries, three hundred county jails and houses of correction, more than five hundred almshouses and other institutions, besides hospitals and houses of refuge," she said.

Although middle-aged, in ill health and susceptible to malaria, she continued her relentless crusade.

From 1841 to 1845 three hospitals for the mentally ill were expanded or founded because of her efforts, among them the Worcester State Hospital in Massachusetts, the Butler Hospital in Rhode Island, a hospital in Utica, New

York, and three new hospitals in Trenton, New Jersey; Harrisburg, Pennsylvania; and Toronto, Canada.

Every year a new asylum was established because of her. She was particularly favored in the South, because she was not political, controversial or demanding. She never attacked slavery, which was a predominant issue among her fellow reformers of the times.

Her first and only concern was the humane treatment of the insane, and because of her resolute character, she became the first New England reformer and first woman to achieve dramatic changes in the southern states. Because of her efforts, nine southern states established mental institutions based on her research and subsequent pleas before southern legislatures.

From 1845 to 1852, she convinced the legislative bodies of Indiana, Illinois, Kentucky, Tennessee, Missouri, Mississippi, Louisiana, Alabama, North and South Carolina and Maryland to establish hospitals for the care and treatment of the mentally ill.

In 1848, she took her cause to the United States Congress. She presented a national memorial to the Congress requesting twelve million acres of land to be used throughout the country for establishing mental institutions.

"I myself have seen more than nine thousand idiots, epileptics, and the insane in these Untied States, destitute of appropriate care and protection," she told Congress.

Congress had given land to each state to be used for highways, schools, railroads and other public needs. She argued that the care and treatment of the mentally ill constituted a similar public need.

For six years her Congressional appeal languished, but finally in 1854, with her national reputation at its peak and public sentiment behind her, a bill based on her request passed both houses of Congress.

The bill called for twelve million acres of land to be allocated throughout the country for the treatment of the mentally ill, and also for the creation of a Washington, D.C., hospital that would care for the mentally ill within the ranks of the United States army and navy.

Although she had been promised support by President Franklin Pierce, he vetoed the bill, arguing that Congress could only designate charitable provisions for the care of the mentally ill within the confines of the capital. Pierce maintained that if Congress helped all the indigent mentally ill people in the country, the government would be called upon to help all the poor and destitute throughout the country.

Following the defeat of her national appeal, exhausted and disappointed by Pierce's inaction, she traveled abroad, to recuperate and to continue her crusade. She traveled first to England and later throughout Europe. She remained constantly active raising funds for her crusade and speaking out on behalf of the mentally ill.

Queen Victoria, at her urging, established a commission to study the condition of the mentally ill in Scotland. Her work in Italy led to the establishment of a hospital for the mentally ill in Rome.

While she was abroad, America was inching toward Civil War.

In 1861, now back in America, she volunteered her services. She was appointed Superintendent of Woman Nurses by the Surgeon General, with the responsibility of assigning women nurses to all Union hospitals and military facilities.

She set about recruiting competent and mature nurses and weeding out those she felt were merely romantic adventurers. Soon, however, controversy enveloped her appointment.

First she refused to accept qualified nursing nuns and other members of religious orders. She abruptly barred all applicants younger than thirty years old and ordered that "All nurses are required to be plain-looking women."

Because she was so used to working alone and independently, she found it hard to operate within the bureaucratic confines of the Federal government.

During the course of the Civil War, she tried to do everything by herself, from inspecting hospitals to distributing supplies. She set up infirmaries and sewing circles, wrote to the parents of wounded soldiers, and collected and distributed provisions. Working endlessly, her health and mental condition began to fail.

It was the most frustrating and disappointing period in her long career. She was under constant criticism for her relentless pursuit of perfection. The friction between her and doctors and nurses serving in the field grew so intense that in 1863 her duties were curtailed.

"This is not the work I would have my life judged by," she said. But she remained faithfully in her position until 1866 and finally retired from government service.

When the war ended and she was asked how the country could best repay her for her noble service, she requested only a pair of Union flags, which were presented to her by the Secretary of War, Edwin Stanton.

After the war she worked to get pensions for veterans and financial compensation for military nurses. She resumed her visits to hospitals and prisons, particularly in the South, which had been ravaged by the war.

Although most Americans agreed that a national monument should be erected for those who gave their lives in the Civil War, no one wanted to attempt the task—except Dorothea.

She personally searched through the granite quarries in Maine for the right-sized rock and oversaw the project until the monument was erected at the National Cemetery in Virginia.

In October 1881, at seventy-nine, she retired to the Trenton, New Jersey, state hospital that she had helped establish some thirty-five years before.

Although her health was failing rapidly, her desire to serve never diminished.

"I think even lying in my bed I can still do something," she said.

When she began her crusade for the mentally ill in the 1840s there were a mere thirteen mental institutions in the country. By 1880, there were 123.

Her efforts, especially in later life during the course of the Civil War, have been ridiculed.

"She is a kind old soul, but very queer and arbitrary," wrote Louisa May Alcott of Dorothea's endeavors during the Civil War.

Yet, contrary to this observation, one of her earliest biographers, Frances Tiffany, wrote in 1890 that "To find her parallel in this respect, it is necessary to go back to the lives of such memorable Roman Catholic women as St. Theresa of Spain or Santa Chiara of Assisi."

Dorothea lived on in the confines of the Trenton hospital for six years following her retirement, and despite ill health and failing faculties, she managed to meet with visitors and friends.

"Rather than emblazon it on monuments of stone, her name was written in the hearts of the generations that knew her, and with their passing, her place in social history has been overlooked," wrote another biographer, Helen Marshall.

Dorothea Dix died at the hospital in 1887, and is buried in Mount Auburn Cemetery in Cambridge, Massachusetts.

Suggested Reading

Baker, Rachel. *Angel of Mercy* (1955).
Beach, Seth. *Daughters of the Puritans* (1905).
Lowe, Corinne. *The Gentle Warrior* (1948).
Schlaifer, Charlene. *Heart's Work* (1991).
Wilson, Dorothy. *Strangers and Travelers: The Story of Dorothea Dix* (1975).

6 KINDERGARTEN CULTURE
Elizabeth Peabody, 1804–1894

"Every human cause had her sympathy and man her active aid."

PEOPLE, PLACES AND EVENTS: Education in America, especially for young children, was one of the country's earliest priorities. This notion was not propelled by any secular reason, but rather by the desire that everyone be able to read and understand the Bible.

The first schoolmaster in the country, Adam Roelantsen, established the first school in America in New York in 1633.

In that same year, the first secondary educational school, the Boston Latin School, was established. It is still functioning today, making it the oldest secondary education school in America.

In 1647, the first public education law was passed in Massachusetts, directing every community of fifty or more households to establish free elementary education. Communities with 100 or more households were required to provide free secondary education as well. By 1720, there were five public schools in Boston.

Seven colleges were established in the country before the American Revolution, including Harvard, The College of

William and Mary, Yale, Princeton, Columbia, Brown and Rutgers.

By 1810 the number of colleges in the country had grown to 37. The yearly tuition at Harvard in the early 1800s was $300.

During the pre-Civil War years, most teachers in public schools were women. In Boston, 6,000 of the 8,000 teachers employed were women.

The first kindergarten was opened in Watertown, Wisconsin, in 1856. It was a German-speaking school.

Four years later, the first English-speaking kindergarten was established in Boston by Elizabeth Peabody.

Both these early institutions of learning followed the teachings of German educator Friedrich Frobel, known as the "Father of Kindergartening."

Kindergartens flourished throughout mid-nineteenth century New England, but mostly for the children of America's privileged classes.

It was not until several decades later that Dr. Maria Montessori, working with underprivileged children in Italy, discovered that preschool education was beneficial to children of all social and economic classes.

Over the past 135 years, the work of early educators like Friedrich Frobel in Germany and Elizabeth Peabody in New England has proven invaluable to the development of American education.

*****

Kindergarten, one of the most far-reaching developments in American education and the first contact most children have with America's vast and complex learning process, was begun in the United States by Elizabeth Peabody, a woman who ironically had no children of her own.

She was born in Billerica, Massachusetts, in 1804 and began the first American kindergarten on Pickney Street in Boston in 1860.

She was the oldest of seven children. Her father, Nathaniel, was a teacher at Phillips Andover Academy, and later became a dentist when the Peabody family moved to Salem, Massachusetts.

Her mother, Elizabeth, taught school in Salem. It was from her mother that young Elizabeth absorbed her educational philosophy.

Her mother's guiding educational principle was that every child should receive an education that would prepare that child to be a genius. It was a noble, although naïve, undertaking.

Elizabeth was educated at her mother's school, and through advanced tutoring developed a keen interest in philosophy, theology, history and literature.

When she was just a teenager, she taught in her mother's school, and later in Boston. She ultimately went to Maine where she served as a governess.

"Kindergartening," she wrote in *Kindergarten Culture*, one of her many books on early childhood education, "is not a craft, it is a religion; not an avocation, but a vocation ... ."

Although she can be credited with starting the first kindergarten, it was her writings and lectures that most contributed to establishing the kindergarten system throughout America.

Peabody's interest in kindergartens came from reading the works of Friedich Frobel. Frobel believed that play was the basic form of self-expression. Although assailed by critics during his lifetime, his work profoundly influenced educators worldwide.

Peabody became devoted to Frobel's principle of creative play in early childhood education and made it her life work.

In 1867, wanting to learn more about Frobel's teachings, she traveled to Germany, visiting established kindergartens and studying with the people who had known Frobel.

After her return to America, she declared that her Pickney Street kindergarten was a failure because it did not adhere to Frobel's teachings. She subsequently closed the school.

While Elizabeth was in Germany, a genuine kindergarten was established in Boston under the direction of her older sister, Mary.

Mary Peabody Mann was the wife of America's most renowned educator, Horace Mann. Mann was famous for promoting public education for all children and for raising the standards of education throughout the country.

In 1863, Mary wrote *Moral Culture of Infancy, and Kindergarten Guide* with her sister, and the book became a Bible for children's educational reform.

The Peabody sisters, Mary, Sophia and Elizabeth, all left their mark on American society. Sophia Peabody married Nathaniel Hawthorne, one of America's literary giants. He was the author of *The Scarlet Letter* and *The House of the Seven Gables*, both considered American literary masterpieces.

Elizabeth devoted herself to writing and lecturing on the importance and structure of kindergarten education. She published *The Kindergarten Messenger*, an independent journal on education reform, as well as numerous books, including *The Kindergarten Culture* (1870) and *Letters to Kindergarteners* (1886). She traveled extensively throughout the country promoting the establishment of kindergartens.

Although the first publicly financed kindergarten in Boston failed after four short years, due primarily to the lack of public appropriations, Elizabeth did not curtail her efforts. Ultimately, kindergartens, both publicly and privately financed, sprang up across the country.

Elizabeth taught at Bronson Alcott's progressive Temple School in Boston. Alcott was both a progressive educator and a Transcendentalist philosopher. His innovations in education did not catch on with the public and the Temple School eventually closed.

Elizabeth recorded her experience at the Temple School in her book, *Record of a School* (1835). After leaving the Temple School, she became active in adult education in Boston, where she taught history at various schools.

Before becoming the leading advocate of kindergarten education, she was an integral part of what is referred to as the golden age of literature and philosophy in Boston.

In 1839 she opened a bookstore on West Street which became the gathering place for many of America's greatest minds, among them authors Margaret Fuller and Nathaniel Hawthorne, social philosophers Ralph Waldo Emerson and Henry David Thoreau, educator Horace Mann, theologians William Channing and Theodore Parker, and Julia Ward Howe, author of the "Battle Hymn of the Republic."

Many foreign books, magazines, and newspapers previously unavailable in the country appeared on the shelves in her bookstore. On Wednesday evenings, the bookstore became a meeting place for the Transcendentalists.

Transcendentalism flourished in New England from 1835 until 1860. The Transcendentalists believed in the divinity and unity of mankind and nature. They believed that man's internal intuition took precedent over perception and man-made laws, and that all mankind answered to a higher authority than government.

Elizabeth Peabody, along with Margaret Fuller, was one of the leading women in this movement.

It was at her bookstore that the ideas for *Dial*, one of America's most influential Transcendental magazines, took form, as well as the idea for Brook Farm, one of America's first utopian living experiments, founded by George Ripley.

Along with the bookstore, Peabody established herself as the first woman publisher in Boston. Her publishing efforts produced a host of antislavery literature, three children's books written by Nathaniel Hawthorne, and publication of *Dial*. In 1849 she published the one and only issue of her own Transcendentalist magazine, *Æsthetic Papers*.

It was in this magazine that Henry David Thoreau's far-reaching essay, "Civil Disobedience," was first published. This essay went on to become a literary and social landmark, the foundation for Mohandas Gandi's independence movement in India, and Martin Luther King's civil rights movement in America.

Peabody wrote that "The final cause of human society is the unfolding of the individual man into every form of perfection, without let or hindrance, according to the inward nature of each."

In her article, "A Glimpse of Christ's Idea of Society," published in the October 1841 issue of *Dial*, she wrote that the essential reform needed to bring about the ideal society was mankind's "educating its children truly."

In later years, the cause of Christianity-based Transcendental education for children became the primary passion in her life. When the Transcendental movement in America began to ebb, she closed her bookstore.

All energies then went into writing and lecturing on education reform. Between 1850 and 1884, she wrote ten books and an estimated fifty articles on the subject.

She gave up what many considered a promising literary career when she made education her calling. Moncure Conway, a noted journalist of the period, wrote, "Miss Peabody's devotion to kindergartens is one of the great literary tragedies. She could be one of the great women of letters in America."

To this, Peabody responded, "Is it not better to make men and women, than to make books?"

In later life, she became an outspoken advocate of native American rights, and her last few public speaking engagements were pleas for justice for native Americans.

In time, she became the object of gossip because of her eccentric behavior. Plagued by failing eyesight, a weight problem, and lack of money, she often neglected the formalities of normal everyday living. According to Lucy Wheelock, a kindergarten teacher who accompanied Peabody on many speaking engagements around the country, she often traveled with her toothbrush in her handbag and wore her nightgown beneath her dress.

It is rumored that Henry James used her as the model for the character Miss Birdseye in his novel *The Bostonians*, although he denied it.

She died at her home in Boston in 1894 at the age of ninety. She is buried in Sleepy Hollow Cemetery in Concord, Massachusetts, the same cemetery where Ralph Waldo Emerson and her brother-in-law, Nathaniel Hawthorne, lie.

Her epitaph reads "A teacher of three generations of children and founder of the kindergarten in America. Every human cause had her sympathy and man her active aid."

Suggested Reading

Baylor, Ruth. *Elizabeth Peabody, Kindergarten Pioneer* (1965).
Brookes, Gladys. *Three Wise Virgins* (1957).
Hoyt, Edwin. *The Peabody Influence* (1968).
Peabody, Elizabeth. *The Letters of Elizabeth Palmer Peabody* (1984).
Tharp, Louise. *The Peabody Sisters of Salem* (1950).

7 THE LITTLE WOMAN WHO MADE A BIG WAR
Harriet Beecher Stowe, 1811–1896

"The Lord Himself wrote it. I was but an instrument in his hand."

PEOPLE, PLACES AND EVENTS: Slavery was one of the first monumental social issues in America in which woman played an important and influential role.

Harriet Beecher Stowe's novel *Uncle Tom's Cabin* influenced the nation's consciousness of slavery.

Anna Elizabeth Dickinson became the major campaign speaker in President Abraham Lincoln's reelection campaign. In 1864 she became the first woman to address both houses of Congress, pleading for passage of the Freedmen's Relief Fund to aid destitute newly freed Southern slaves.

The national crisis of the Civil War also produced Julia Ward Howe, who, on a visit to Washington, D. C., in 1861, penned the verses to "The Battle Hymn of the Republic," set to the music of an old American folk tune. Her poem was published in 1862 in the Boston-based magazine *The Atlantic Monthly* and instantly became the semiofficial Civil War song of the Union Army.

The Civil War began in the early morning of April 12, 1861, when Confederate forces opened fire on Fort Sumter in the harbor at Charleston, South Carolina. In February the Confederate States of America, made up of eleven slave-holding states, was formed in Alabama, and Jefferson Davis of Mississippi was elected President.

The population of the country was nearly thirty-two million. There were thirty-three states in the Union. The Civil War lasted four years. There were more than 2,000 battles. More than 600,000 men on both sides were killed and twice that many were wounded.

The war ended on April 9, 1865, when General Robert E. Lee, commander of the Confederate forces, surrendered to General Ulysses S. Grant, commander of the Union troops, at Appomattox Courthouse in Virginia.

Six days after the end of the war, President Lincoln was assassinated.

* * * * *

No New England woman or book made more of a dramatic impact on American culture and society than Litchfield, Connecticut's, Harriet Beecher Stowe, the author of *Uncle Tom's Cabin*.

Her novel, published in 1852, was one of the most popular and influential novels ever written by an American author, and one that helped precipitate the American Civil War. On a visit to the White House, President Abraham Lincoln reportedly greeted Mrs. Stowe as "The little woman who wrote the book that made this big war."

There were obviously far more complex and far-reaching causes for the Civil War, but there is no doubt that the publication of her book provided immense influence in defining the anti-slavery role of the North against the slave-holding states of the South.

"By arousing the general sentiment of the world against slavery, the novel contributed more than any other one thing to its abolition in that generation, and did more than any one thing that ever occurred to precipitate the war," wrote Southern writer Thomas Nelson Page.

No other book in publishing history was more topical or psychologically attuned to the divisions within the country. The vast reading audience of the book, which sold more than 300,000 copies the first year of its publication, was more than ready for Mrs. Stowe's explosive story.

The debate over the issue of slavery at the time of the book's publication in 1852 had grown volatile. (The book was first serialized from 1851 through 1852 in *National Era*, an anti-slavery newspaper based in Washington, D.C.) For nearly twenty years Northern abolitionists had kept up anti-slavery agitation, and the issue was the most dominant controversy in America.

The bitterness between the Northern and Southern states had intensified with the passage of the Fugitive Slave Law of 1850, which allowed Southern slave owners to pursue and recapture runaway slaves even in non-slave holding states in the North.

Its publication sparked even more controversy among Southern reviewers and lawmakers. One Southern reviewer hailed the book as "a monstrous distortion inspired by Abolitionist fanaticism and designed to excite sectional discord."

Another reviewer said, "Uncle Tom's Cabin has done more harm to the world than any other book ever written."

In contrast, Northern reviewers, like William Lloyd Garrison, publisher of the anti-slavery publication *Liberator*, said the book would have "a prodigious effect upon all intelligent and human minds."

The most popular American poet of the times, Henry Wadsworth Longfellow, wrote to Mrs. Stowe, saying, "I congratulate you most cordially upon the immense success and influence of Uncle Tom's Cabin. It is one of the greatest triumphs recorded in literary history, to say nothing of the higher triumph of its moral effects."

Ironically, Mrs. Stowe never intended her book to divide the country. She deliberately made the villain of the novel, Simon Legree, a transplanted New Englander (from Vermont) and she expected to be attacked more severely by Northerners because she maintained that they had tolerated slavery when there was no economic or cultural reason to.

The book has a simple premise, telling the stories of Uncle Tom, a middle-aged, intelligent and deeply religious black man, and Eliza, a young woman slave.

Eliza escapes from slavery when she flees with her son across the Ohio River from Kentucky, and is helped by Quakers and other sympathetic whites. She eventually escapes to Canada and finally back to Africa with her son and husband.

Uncle Tom, who refuses to run away, tries to save the life of his master's daughter. Because of his heroic attempt his master sets him free, but before Uncle Tom can leave, his master dies, and Uncle Tom is sold to a brutal drunkard, Simon Legree. Tom can never appease his new master, and finally Legree, a former New Englander, beats Uncle Tom to death.

Mrs Stowe had intended her book to address Southern readers and she hoped it would reconcile the differences between both parts of the country and avert a pending war.

In a letter to a friend discussing the reasons why she wrote the book, she explained her intent was to "soften and moderate the bitterness of feeling in extreme abolitionists; to convert to abolitionists views many whom this same bitterness had repelled; to inspire the free colored people with self respect, hope and confidence," and "to inspire universally through the country a kindlier feeling toward the Negro race."

A tidal wave of criticism washed over her work from both Northern and Southern pro-slavery proponents. She received thousands of angry letters. In the South, some courts were sentencing people to jail for simply having the book in their possession.

Southern magazines and newspapers denounced her work, saying it unfairly portrayed the issue of slavery, and because of her self-righteous tone, and coming from New England, she was addressing issues that she knew nothing about.

Critics of the book maintained that she had no knowledge of the Southern laws governing the treatment of slaves or of Southern culture and customs. The general denunciation of the book maintained that most slaves were happy and content, and that her assumption that slaves were intellectually and morally equal to white people was ludicrous.

A flood of anti-Uncle Tom books were published to dispute Mrs. Stowes' book. Most were novels, and all of them supported slavery and condemned the abolitionist movement. None, however, were as successful and influential as *Uncle Tom's Cabin*.

Criticism of the book was not limited solely to the United States. A London Times editorial said, "Let us have no more Uncle Tom's Cabins' engendering ill will and keeping up bad blood."

Born in Litchfield, Connecticut, in 1811, Harriet Beecher was the daughter of a well known and highly regarded New England Presbyterian minister, Lyman Beecher. She was one of thirteen children. Six of her brothers became clergymen.

Her education was religious by nature, although she studied the classics as well. When she was twenty-one years old, the family left New England and moved to Cincinnati, where her father became the president of the Lane Theological Seminary. In Cincinnati, she met and married Calvin Stowe, a professor and minister.

It was in Cincinnati that she first learned about slavery. The city was located just across the Ohio River from slave-holding plantations in Kentucky.

Anti-abolitionist rallies were held everywhere in the city. It was the heart of an ongoing slavery debate, both pro and con. The city was also a refuge for slaves escaping North to Canada.

The seminary where her father served as president was a center of anti-slavery debate. Her home also served as a shelter for runaway slaves that her father hid from authorities.

It was there that she heard first-hand accounts of cruelty and abuse at the hands of slave owners. The slaves filled her with stories of broken families, torture and the horrors of slavery.

In 1850, her husband was given a job as a professor at Bowdoin College in Maine. Harriet, Calvin and their six children all moved to Brunswick.

Settled back in New England, she turned her attentions to writing. She had always had a talent for writing and had previously published several stories and articles in small publications.

At the urging of her family, she undertook the task of writing a book that she hoped would expose the tyranny of slavery. Her sister-in-law, Isabel, wrote to her urging her to write a book that "will make this whole nation feel what an accursed thing slavery is."

According to a biography of Mrs. Stowe, written by her son, Charles, the inspiration for *Uncle Tom's Cabin* came to his mother during a church service.

According to his account, "suddenly, like the unrolling of a picture, the scene of the death of Uncle Tom passed before her mind. So strongly was she affected that it was with difficulty she could keep from weeping aloud. Immediately on returning home she took out pen and paper and wrote out the vision which had been as it were blown into her mind as by the rushing of a mighty wind."

This last chapter of the famous book was written first, in a frenzy. She once insisted that "the Lord Himself wrote it. I was but an instrument in his hand."

She read the chapter to her husband and children. Her husband, who was deeply touched by what his wife had written, told her, "This is the climax of that story of slavery which you promised sister Isabel you would write. Begin at the beginning and work up to this and you'll have your book."

In early 1851 she began writing. She wrote to Gamaliel Bailey, editor of *National Era*, asking if he would be interested in publishing the work. Bailey had known the Beecher family in Cincinnati, where he had been publishing another anti-slavery journal. He was driven out of Cincinnati by anti-abolitionist mobs.

Although *National Era*'s circulation was small, it had a devoted following. Bailey offered Mrs. Stowe $300 for the manuscript, which he agreed to publish in serial form beginning in June 1851. She intended the book to take only a month to complete, but instead her weekly installments in *National Era* went on for nearly a year.

She had told Bailey that the work would include "a series of sketches which give the lights and shadows of the patriarchal institution, written either from observation, incidents which have occurred in the sphere of my personal knowledge, or in the knowledge of my friends."

The book's serial publication caused an immediate uproar.

"We do not recollect any production of an American writer that has excited more general and profound interest," Mr. Bailey wrote at the end of the serialization.

After its serialization, the book was turned down by the first publisher Mrs. Stowe approached with it. The publisher feared alienating his Southern customers.

Finally, Boston publisher John P. Jewett agreed to publish the work, but asked her to share the printing costs as well as the profits. Mrs. Stowe was not interested in investing in the publishing endeavor, and instead agreed to take a straight ten-percent royalty. It turned out to be a decision that cost her a fortune, since the book sales went into the millions.

The book appeared in two volumes. The original edition was five thousand copies. Three thousand copies of the book sold on the first day and the rest the very next day. Within a month a second edition sold out.

Within five years millions of copies had been sold throughout the country and in England. More than twenty editions of the book were published in London alone, none of which paid any royalties to Mrs. Stowe.

The book was afforded a popular reception never before given to a novel. Copies were published throughout Europe.

The novel was dramatized, and became one of the most popular plays produced for the stage. Thousands of theater groups throughout the country produced the play, from which Mrs. Stowe again received no financial reward. The copyright laws in the 1850s did not cover dramatizations.

She did not approve of the plays based on her book, but she had no control over the productions. She never authorized any production company to dramatize her book.

The popularity of *Uncle Tom's Cabin* was immense and far-reaching. Its publication in terms of sheer numbers surpasses anything in the history of publishing, and only the

Bible is believed to have outsold it. Its circulation was worldwide and its impact, in terms of American history and culture, was immediate and lasting.

One of the immediate effects of its publication was to make the enforcement of the Fugitive Slave Law impossible. The book raised the consciousness of most Northerners who almost uniformly decided not to cooperate with the law.

Because of the book, Northerners came to recognize the evil of slavery and even those who were previously undecided about the issue soon came to realize the immorality of the slave business.

The literary merits of the book have long been overshadowed by the cultural impact it had. Critics have long debated its merit almost as vehemently as its politics.

"The style is commonplace, the language is often trite and inelegant, sometimes degenerating into slang; and the humor is strained," historian James Ford Rhodes wrote about the book's style.

A Southern literary critic noted that "She has seen plenty of blacks but cannot make them talk. Her ear is impossible; she has no sense of their rhythm or vividness."

Other critics noted that despite its power as a "great human document," the book had "blemishes of structure and sentimentalism."

According to another critic, Mrs. Stowe "was the first American writer to take the Negro seriously and to conceive a novel with a black man as the hero."

Whatever its literary merits, the book stands as one of America's most significant sociological documents.

Its publication made her an instant international celebrity. The year after the book appeared she made her first of three trips abroad, visiting England and Scotland. She was received by Queen Victoria and met with England's foremost author, Charles Dickens. No American author ever created as much excitement.

Years later, when the South had seceded, Queen Victoria declared her country's neutrality, but England depended on the South's cotton for its cotton mills, which went idle.

Given the economic dangers faced by her country, the Queen then threatened to recognize the Confederacy.

This time, Mrs. Stowe wrote an open letter to the 500,000 British women who had signed and sent her an "Affectionate and Christian Address," following the publication of Uncle Tom's Cabin.

"We say to you sisters, you have spoken well; we have heard you; we have heeded; we have striven in the cause, even unto death ... . In many of our dwellings the very light of our lives have gone out; and yet we accept the life-long darkness as our part of this great and awful expiation, by which the bonds of wickedness shall be loosed, and abiding peace established on the foundation of righteousness. Sisters, what have you done, and what do you mean to do?"

In January 1863, the Boston-based magazine *The Atlantic Monthly* published her letter, and copies of it were sent to England, where it became a driving abolitionist force.

Publication of her letter inspired anti-slavery rallies throughout England, and the outpouring of public sentiment against slavery neutralized all talk of England recognizing the Confederacy. President Lincoln credited her letter to the women of England as being among the reasons why England did not enter the war.

She wrote only one other book about slavery, *Dred, A Tale of the Great Dismal Swamp*, published in 1856. In four weeks, the book sold 100,000 copies, but it never approached the popularity or sales of *Uncle Tom's Cabin*.

She spent a great part of her later life in Florida, where she bought a small plantation along the banks of the St.

John's River. One of her sons, who had been wounded at the battle of Gettysburg, became a planter there and she worked with freed slaves, helping them adapt to Reconstruction.

She spent her remaining years in Hartford, Connecticut, where she wrote articles, stories and serialized novels, many of which appeared in *The Atlantic Monthly*. Among her other books were *The Pearl of Orr's Island* (1862), *Oldtown Folks* (1869), *Poganuc People* (1878) and *A Dog's Mission* (1881).

In 1869 she published a controversial article in *The Atlantic Monthly* in which she alleged that poet Lord Byron had had an incestuous affair with his half-sister. The article caused an uproar and cost her some of her noted popularity. Still, she remained a leading American author and lecturer until her death at the age of eighty-five in 1896.

Suggested Reading

Adams, John. *Harriet Beecher Stowe* (1963).
Billington, Ray Allen. *American History Before 1877* (1965).
Crozier, Alice. *The Novels of Harriet Beecher Stowe* (1969).
Moers, Ellen. *Harriet Beecher Stowe and American Literature* (1978).
Spiller, Robert E., Willard Thorp, Thomas H. Johnson and Henry Seidel Canby. *Literary History of the United States* (1946).

8 FIELD OF THE HEAVENS
Maria Mitchell, 1818–1889

"The landscape is flat and somewhat monotonous and the field of the heavens has greater attraction."

PEOPLE, PLACES AND EVENTS: New England women have always been in the forefront of the field of astronomy. Among the many were Mary Whitney, Henrietta Leavitt, Williamina Fleming, Annie Cannon and Maria Mitchell.

One of the first major achievements in astronomy in America occurred in 1680 when Boston mathematician Thomas Brattle calculated the orbit of a comet, using Sir Isaac Newton's *Theory of Cometary Orbits*. Newton acknowledged Brattle's discovery.

The first planetarium in the country was built in Philadelphia by David Rittenhouse, who two years later successfully plotted the orbits of the planets Venus and Mercury.

In 1839, the Harvard Observatory was founded by William Bond. Bond began the observatory in his home, and later moved the facility onto the Cambridge, Massachusetts, campus.

In 1843, the Observatory acquired, through substantial donations, the largest telescope in the country and the most sophisticated astronomical equipment in the world, making it the hub of astronomical investigation.

Henrietta Leavitt, who was born in Lancaster, Massachusetts, and grew up in Cambridge (1868–1921), worked at the Harvard Observatory and was a driving force in the analysis of the magnitude of stars. She was instrumental in the development of *The Astrographic Map of the Sky*, completed in 1913.

Although born in Scotland, Williamina Fleming (1857–1911) moved to Massachusetts when she married a Bostonian, and served at the Harvard Observatory under Edward C. Pickering, professor of astronomy and director of the observatory. Her distinguished contributions there led to her appointment in 1906 to the Royal Astronomical Society, the first woman ever elected to the prestigious organization.

Annie Cannon (1863–1941) was born in Delaware and attended Wellesley and Radcliffe colleges. In 1896, she served at Harvard, working with Williamina Fleming, where she helped classify more than 200,000 stars. Her work was published in the nine-volume work, *The Henry Draper Catalogue*. She was also the first woman awarded an honorary doctorate from Oxford University.

Mary Whitney (1847–1921) was born in Waltham, Massachusetts, and attended Vassar, where she became Maria Mitchell's assistant. In 1888, she succeeded Mitchell as professor of astronomy at the college and director of the Vassar Observatory. In 1899 she helped found the American Astronomical Society.

*****

Nantucket Island's Maria Mitchell had an astronomical career—quite literally. The young nineteenth-century Quaker woman gained worldwide recognition, despite great odds, for her discovery of the comet of 1847, commonly known as "Miss Mitchell's Comet."

In 1848, at the age of twenty-nine, she became the first American and first woman ever to be awarded a gold medal for astronomy by the King of Denmark. In the same year, she became the first woman elected to the American Academy of Arts and Sciences.

She went on to become the first professor of astronomy at Vassar College in Poughkeepsie, New York, a position she held until she retired in 1888 at age sixty-nine.

The twin elements of religion and commerce shaped Nantucket Island's destiny and influenced Mitchell's destiny as well. For over a century, Quakerism was not only the dominant force in the island's religious life, but in its social and economic affairs as well. In no other community in the world did Quakers compose such a large proportion of the citizenry.

The whaling industry was the second greatest influence on island life. Nantucket Islanders were not the first colonial whalers, but because of the island's proximity to the migratory routes of the whales, and because of the vast markets in Boston and New York for whale oil, the industry gave birth (from 1820 to 1850) to a new and powerful economic force on the island.

In 1818, Maria Mitchell was born on Nantucket Island, one of nine children born to William and Lydia Mitchell. William was a schoolteacher forced into the whaling industry to provide for his family. His wife was the island librarian.

An avid reader as a child, Maria had read most of her father's history and science books by the time she was ten years old. She often accompanied her father on long nature walks across the island where he taught her about the beauty and wonders of the environment.

"Thee must watch closely, then will thee see and know for thyself," William Mitchell taught his young daughter.

It was from her father that Maria developed a deep passion for the world's natural beauty and understanding of the physical laws of nature. Of all her studies, mathematics and astronomy most intrigued her.

Perhaps in other parts of the country during the nineteenth century, her fascination with astronomy might have been discouraged, but because she grew up in a whaling port, knowledge of the stars and the uses of a sextant and telescope were considered natural.

When asked years later why she was drawn to astronomy, she said, "It was, in the first place, a love of mathematics, seconded by my sympathy with my father's love for astronomical observation. But the spirit of the place had also much to do with it.

"In Nantucket, people quite generally are in the habit of observing the heavens and a sextant will be found in almost every house. The landscape is flat and somewhat monotonous and the field of the heavens has greater attraction ... ."

In 1830, Maria attended the island public school, where she was considered a rebellious student. Her teachers did not know what to do with her, since she was constantly questioning everything they taught her. Ultimately, she was sent home because of her behavior, so her father decided to begin his own school, where Maria became his prize pupil.

In 1834, when Maria was sixteen years old, her younger sister Eliza became sick. Maria started a school of her own to help pay her family's considerable medical bills. She began classes in reading, spelling, geography, history and math, in a one-room schoolhouse.

Although she was apprehensive about the opening of the school, all her fears disappeared when the classroom filled up with students. Most of the students were Portuguese, and some were black. Many of the black students came to Maria's school after being turned away from the island's public school. Maria accepted them all.

Despite the success of the school, the Mitchell's financial condition grew worse. William Mitchell was on the verge of signing on for a three-year whaling voyage in order to meet the family's expenses, when miraculously, he was offered the position of president of the Island Pacific Bank on Nantucket—a position he readily accepted. The Mitchell family's financial woes were over.

In 1836, the family moved from their small home on Vestal Street to one of the most stately mansions on the island, a large brick house on Main Street that also housed the bank. After moving into the new house, Maria persuaded her father to build a wooden observatory on top of the bank building.

William Mitchell used his influence to persuade the Coast Survey Institute at the West Point Academy to loan Maria some sophisticated observation equipment, including a four-inch equatorial telescope. The agreement was that Maria would use the equipment to chart the heavens as part of a network of Coastal Survey observers. With the observatory built and the new equipment in place, Maria and her father spent each evening sweeping the sky with her telescope and meticulously recording the movement of the stars.

Besides building the observatory for Maria, William Mitchell bought a grand piano for his new home. The Mitchell children all played, and Maria's sickly sister Eliza was comforted by the music. But music of any sort was forbidden by the Quakers. The Quaker Elders demanded that William get rid of the piano, which he did to appease them, despite his children's protests.

On an island ruled by Quaker laws, Maria's nonconformity turned out to be disastrous. In 1840, Eliza died. Overcome with grief at her funeral and unable to bear the hollow blessings of the Quaker Elders, Maria fled the funeral in tears. Because of her behavior, the Elders questioned Maria's commitment to the Quaker faith.

After her sister's death and because of her vast knowledge of mathematics and science, Maria was not able to reconcile the uncompromising teachings of the Quakers with what she knew to be the true laws of nature. When she spoke her mind to the Elders, she was disowned.

Her father remained steadfastly loyal to his rebellious daughter, and when his loyalty was also called into question by the Elders, he also left the organized Quaker religion. After the death of her younger sister and the confrontation with the Elders, Maria buried herself in her work at the observatory. Each night she plotted the course of the stars, keeping her records.

On a warm July night in 1846, Maria awoke to discover the huge steeple of the Methodist Church across the street ablaze, flames shooting into the sky. Fed by the casks of whale oil stored along the wharf at the end of the street, the fire was spreading through the streets.

Maria and her father joined in the fire brigades but the flames were spreading too fast to be contained. The entire town was lost in the blaze. Maria's small observatory atop the bank and all her equipment burned in the fire, along with Maria's notes and records. Heartbroken, but not deterred, Maria and her father rebuilt their home and the observatory.

A little more than a year later, on October 1, 1847, at half past ten in the evening, while making her nightly observations, Maria discovered the trail of a comet, five degrees above Polaris. She scribbled the position of the comet and the time of her observation into her notebook. She immediately awoke her father so he too could view her discovery.

After comparing the celestial object with the stars nearest it and a map of the heavens, he cried, "It is! There was never a star, never a nebula in that place before."

Maria had discovered a new comet.

Although overflowing with excitement at the possibility, Maria remained fearful that the starry blur might eventually turn into a cosmic ghost that frequently appeared in the heavens. It didn't. She continued to plot the course of the comet over the next several days until finally there was no doubt. She had discovered her first comet in the fields of the heavens over Nantucket Island.

William Mitchell wasted no time writing to George Bond, the director of the Harvard University Observatory, to lay claim to his daughter's discovery. In 1831, the King of Denmark, Frederic VI, promised a gold medal award to anyone who discovered a new comet. The conditions of the award were difficult. The medal was to be awarded only to the person who first recorded the sighting.

Although Maria sighted the comet on Oct. 1, an Italian astronomer had also recorded the sighting, but on Oct. 3. Despite the fact that William Mitchell had contacted the Harvard Observatory immediately, his letter did not reach the university until Oct. 4. By then, the Italian astronomer had already claimed the discovery as his own.

Maria and her father traveled to Cambridge, Massachusetts, to meet with George Bond and argue their case. Bond was impressed with Maria's expert documentation of the discovery. He agreed to represent her claim to the Danish King.

During her stay in Cambridge, Maria impressed even the president of Harvard, Edward Everett, who said of her, "She is a young lady, industrious and vigilant, a good astronomer and mathematician, from a remote island ... . It would be pleasant to have the Nantucket girl carry off the prize from all the graybeards and observatories in Europe."

A year after her discovery, Maria received a letter from the Danish King acknowledging her unquestionable claim to the comet, thereafter called, "Miss Mitchell's Comet."

The gold medal she received was inscribed with the words, "Not in vain do we watch the setting and rising of the stars."

Notices of her discovery and award appeared in newspapers throughout the country. She became a much sought-after celebrity, touring and lecturing across America and Europe. She later received honorary degrees from colleges and universities throughout America.

In 1865, when the women's college, Vassar, was founded, she was approached by Matthew Vassar and asked to become the first professor of astronomy at the college and the first director of the Vassar College Observatory.

Maria and her father moved from Nantucket to Poughkeepsie, New York, where they both lived and worked at the college. She taught at Vassar until she retired in 1888. A year later, at the age of seventy, she passed away.

Suggested Reading

Billington, Ray. *American History Before 1877* (1965).
McPherson, Stephanie. *Rooftop Astronomer* (1990).
Morgan, Helen. *Maria Mitchell: First Lady of American Astronomy* (1977).
Wayne, Bennett. *Women Who Dared to Be Different* (1973).
Wright, Helen. *Sweeper in the Sky* (1949).

9 ANGEL OF THE BATTLEFIELDS
Clara Barton, 1821–1912

"She is known wherever man appreciates humanity."

PEOPLE, PLACES AND EVENTS: At the outbreak of the Civil War (1861), there were no trained military nurses to care for sick or wounded soldiers. Most of these duties were undertaken by convalescing soldiers.

President Lincoln's call for volunteers for the Union Army produced thousands of young recruits from cities and farms, eager to join the Union cause.

Training the raw recruits as soldiers was only half the battle.

Military camps had no decent or appropriate sanitary facilities. Food, often obtained from private companies, was rotten and scarce, and troops lacked the necessary clothes, blankets and other provisions.

Dysentery, scurvy and a host of other diseases killed more soldiers than the enemy did.

Although each military regiment was assigned a field surgeon, he often had to work without the help of a trained nursing staff or adequate medical supplies.

Since there was no ambulance service, most of the wounded had to be cared for in makeshift hospitals on the battlefields.

Almost as soon as Lincoln had put out his call for volunteers, Ladies' Aid Societies began to spring up throughout the North. The groups were organized to collect and distribute needed supplies and provisions to the Union forces. Southern women formed similar groups.

There were several thousand aid societies, all working independently to procure needed clothes, blankets, uniforms and medical supplies.

Dr. Elizabeth Blackwell took it upon herself to create a central coordinating organization to oversee the collective efforts of the societies.

The Women's Central Association directed the efforts of these groups of women helping to collect and distribute mass quantities of needed supplies. Over two million troops were ultimately served through the Association.

The Association convinced government officials of the dire need for trained military nurses to be used in the war effort. The Women's Central Association was given the responsibility of recruiting and training 100 women for this task.

The Association also fought to create a sanitary commission to oversee the inspection of all military camps, prisons and hospitals and provide proper sanitary facilities at all of them.

At the beginning of the war, military surgeons and doctors were skeptical of the women nurses and had them engaged primarily in only the most basic housekeeping tasks. Gradually, as the war wore on, they assumed far more appropriate responsibilities. Their contributions proved indispensable, both on the battlefields and behind the lines at military hospitals.

During the course of the Civil War, nearly 300 women served as surgeons and doctors, while thousands of women served as army nurses. One of the most famous was Clara Barton.

* * * * *

Of all the things Clara Barton learned from her family, it was her brother David teaching her to ride a horse when she was a young girl that meant the most to her.

"Sometimes, in later years, when I found myself on a strange horse, in a troop saddle, flying for life and liberty in front of pursuit, I blessed the baby lessons of the wild gallops among the colts," she said. And her life was filled with many wild gallops on battlefields, ranging from the Civil War to the Franco-Prussian War in Europe.

In her autobiographical book, *Story of My Childhood*, she wrote, "It was David's delight to take me, a little girl five years old, to the field, seize a couple of those beautiful grazing creatures, broken only to the halter and bit, and gathering the reins of both bridles in one hand, throw me on the back of one colt, springing on the other himself ... and gallop away over fields and fen, in and out among the other colts, in wild gless of ourselves."

"Catch hold of his mane, Clara and just feel the horse a part of yourself," her brother told her.

It was also from her brother David that she gained her first experience in nursing, which was to become her lifelong calling. She was only eleven years old when David suffered a blow to the head and was bed-ridden for two years recuperating.

She cared for him day and night throughout those two long years of recovery. Although she had no formal medical training, she taught herself to be resourceful and remain calm and devoted to attending to her brother. These skills stayed with her for a lifetime.

Clara Barton was born on Christmas Day, December 25, 1821, in Oxford, Massachusetts, to Captain Stephen Barton and his wife Sarah. It had been ten years since Sarah Barton had given birth to her last child and the Bartons were overjoyed when Clara was born.

"Now, isn't that the best kind of Christmas gift for all of us?" her father rejoiced.

Stephen Barton was a retired Revolutionary War officer, having served under "Mad Anthony" Wayne. He also served in the Indian Wars following the Revolution.

The new Barton baby was christened "Clarissa Harlowe," named after a well-known fictional heroine of the times, but she quickly became known simply as Clara.

She had four older brothers and sisters. Her oldest sister, Dorothy, was seventeen and her oldest brother, Stephen, was fifteen. Her favorite brother David was thirteen and her sister Sally was ten.

The Barton farmhouse was simple and functional, built on top of hill, overlooking a vast pasture where Captain Barton grazed his thoroughbred horses and colts.

The Bartons were one of Oxford's oldest pioneering families, having helped settle the small town and build the historic first Universalist Church of Oxford.

While growing up, each of the Barton family members took it upon themselves to educate the young girl. Her father taught her about politics and the military.

"I listened breathlessly to his war stories. We made illustrations of soldiers and constructed famous battles and fought them. Every shade of military etiquette was regarded and instilled in me," she said.

Because of her father's teachings, when she later found herself engaged in actual warfare, she always knew military protocol and never addressed a general as a colonel or mistook cavalrymen for foot soldiers.

"When later I was suddenly thrust into the mysteries of war and had to take my place and part of it, I found myself far less a stranger to the conditions than most women, or even ordinary men for that matter," she said.

Her mother taught her household skills, including cooking, which became a valuable skill in later life when Clara not only nursed soldiers at the front, but fed them as well.

When she was not listening to her father's stories about the military, or tending to household chores, she took care of the family's array of animals and pets, which included dogs, cats, cows, ducks, chickens, turkeys and horses.

Her oldest sister Dorothy taught her to read and write, and by the time she was three years old, Clara could read a story to herself and knew geography, arithmetic and spelling.

From her oldest brother, Stephen, she learned mathematics. He often filled her chalk slate with math problems that he posed as games for his youngest sister to play and she became proficient in solving mathematical equations at an early age.

But it was from her brother David that she learned about riding and it was a skill that served her well throughout her long life.

"People say that I must have been born brave," she said. " Why I seem to remember nothing but terrors in my early days. I was a shrinking little bundle of fears—fear of thunder, fear of strange faces, fear of my own strange self."

But, whatever those childhood fears might have been, they did not stop Clara from becoming the most beloved nurse on both American and European battlefields, earning her the title of "Angel of the Battlefields" from the soldiers she cared for.

At fifteen, she became a teacher at a local school. In 1852, after ten years of teaching, she entered the Clinton Liberal Institute in New York to further her own education.

After completion of her studies there, she accepted a teaching position in Bordentown, New Jersey. At the time there were no public schools in the town or the state.

The town had tried unsuccessfully several times to start a school, but the unruly farm students would not attend classes and the teachers that were hired could not control them.

At first the town was hesitant to hire the frail-looking Clara Barton to lead the school. They did not want to throw good money away on an already failed experiment in education.

"Give me three months, and I will teach for free," Clara said.

Because of her offer to teach for free for a three-month trial period, she was allowed to rent an old building in town and began her school with only six students. Within six weeks, as the word spread of her devotion and skills as a teacher, the number of students attending school grew to 600.

Seeing her success, the citizens of Bordentown offered her a regular salary and built an eight-room school house where she served as both teacher and principal.

Within three years public education became a fixture in Bordentown, and the old schoolhouse where she began her experiment in teaching is now the Clara Barton Memorial.

Teaching at Bordentown was her last teaching assignment. Always physically frail, her teaching career came to an end when she had a physical breakdown that left her without a voice. Unable to talk, she was forced to give up teaching and seek complete rest.

In 1853, not able to enjoy her self-imposed recuperation, she decided to seek a position as a copyist in the U.S. Patent Office in Washington, D.C., becoming the first woman to do so. Not only that, Clara received a yearly salary of $1,000, which was equal to the pay received by men in the office.

She had exceptional handwriting. Since the typewriter had not yet been invented, her handwriting skills were a much-sought-after commodity. But the idea that a mere woman could receive equal pay to a man outraged many of the male clerks, who shunned her and undermined her efforts.

At the time, the Patent Office was awash in scandal. Dishonest clerks in the office were accused of copying and selling to the highest bidders the ideas of patent-seekers.

Clara managed to endure the hostile working environment with the same quiet resolve and determination that she displayed in establishing public education in Bordentown.

Because of her honesty and hard work, she was later placed in a position of responsibility and influence within the office, which only further outraged her male counterparts.

When President James Buchanan was elected President (185–1861) Clara was removed from her post at the U.S. Patent Office.

Clara's firing had less to do with her gender than with her political sympathies. With the clouds of civil war looming on the horizon, President Buchanan, a Democrat, remained steadfastly a friend to the slave-owning Southern states. Clara had openly expressed her belief in the Union and the freedom of all individuals.

Political opinions aside, President Buchanan was forced to reappoint her when a public outcry arose demanding her reinstatement because of her professional integrity and honesty.

Four years later, when President Abraham Lincoln (1861–1865) was inaugurated, she left her position at the Patent Office in order to serve the Union cause.

She had saved enough money to live on without having to work, and although she did not know exactly how she might serve her country, she was determined to find a way.

"What is money without a country?" she said.

After Fort Sumter was fired upon on April 12, 1861, by Confederate troops, President Lincoln ordered 75,000 Union troops into service. Massachusetts responded by sending four regiments. One of the regiments was made up of young men from Clara's hometown and nearby communities.

When the 6th Massachusetts Regiment marched through Baltimore on their way to the Capitol, they were fired on by mobs of Southern sympathizers. Four Union soldiers were killed and dozens more wounded. When they finally arrived in Washington, they were met by hundreds of women gathered to care for them. Clara Barton was among them. She recognized many of the young wounded soldiers as former students from her teaching days in Oxford.

Although she was not a medically trained nurse by current standards, she worked tirelessly to ease the pain of the injured soldiers and supply them with food, water and other needed comforts. She spent hours reading aloud to the Massachusetts troops from hometown newspapers that she was able to get. When bandages ran out, she organized women to help tear up sheets.

But working behind the lines as the war progressed was not enough for her. The sight of dead and wounded soldiers compelled her to find other ways to help. She decided that the only place her skills could be best used was on the battlefield itself.

Logic dictated that the sooner troops were cared for, the more likely they would recover. But public sentiment at the time was against the notion of women caring for the wounded on the battlefield.

She petitioned the government many times, arguing that she should be allowed to go to the front to care for the wounded. All her pleas were rejected. Finally, with the numbers of Union dead and wounded mounting, she was finally given permission to go to the battlefield as a nurse.

Her first battle was at Cedar Mouth. More than 8,000 Union soldiers were wounded and nearly 2,000 killed.

She wrote of this first battlefield experience, "Five days and nights with three hours sleep, a narrow escape from capture and some days of getting the wounded in Washington hospitals. If you chance to feel that the position was rough and unseemly for a woman, it was also rough and unseemly for men—but under all lay the life of a nation."

During the course of the Civil War she served in sixteen bloody battles.

Among them were the battles of Fort Wayne, Fredericksburg, Second Bull Run, Charleston, Spottsylvania, Richmond and Antietam.

Soon, her name began to be spoken of with great awe and affection by troops on both sides. She did not limit her care to solely Union troops but tended to wounded Confederate soldiers as well.

She was often seen at night, after a battle was over and the sides retreated, scouring the battlefield with a lantern, fearing that some unfortunate wounded soldier might be lying among the dead. It was the wounded soldiers who gave her the name, "Angel of the Battlefields."

During the course of the war, with food and medical supplies running out, she became increasingly adept at obtaining provisions and dispensing them where needed.

As the Civil War came to an end, President Lincoln received thousands of letters from anxious parents searching for information about their missing sons. There were close to 80,000 troops reported missing and unaccounted for.

With the endorsement of the President, Clara established the Bureau of Records in Washington, where she worked for the next four years tracing and identifying there whereabouts of 20,000 missing soldiers.

It was also during this period in her life that she began lecturing on her experiences during the war, agreeing to give 300 lectures throughout the country.

"I am willing to give my services to relieve suffering, but if I must talk, I insist on being paid well," she said. And she was, but the strenuous lecture series took its toll on her health and once again she found herself physically and emotionally spent.

In 1869, on the advice of her family physician, she traveled to Geneva, Switzerland, to recuperate.

Her stay in Geneva did not go unnoticed. While there, she was petitioned by representatives of the International Committee of the Red Cross Society to enlist her help convincing the United States government to sign the Geneva Convention agreement.

The agreement provided for the unhampered relief and care of wounded soldiers during wartime. It had been signed by all civilized nations except the United States.

Clara was in complete agreement with the goals of the International Red Cross, but before she could begin work lobbying representatives of her own government to sign the Geneva agreement, the Franco-Prussian War began, as a result of the Prussian emperor William I's desire to unify German states. The French Emperor, Napoleon III, fearing domination by Prussia, declared war.

At the urging of members of the International Red Cross organization, Clara once more began caring for wounded soldiers at Prussian military hospitals and at the front. When Prussian troops finally overthrew the revolt in Paris, Clara entered the besieged city, where she distributed food and clothing to the starving Parisians and helped care for the wounded.

At the close of the war in 1871, she was awarded the Iron Cross of Germany for her heroic efforts. She spent several years traveling throughout Europe as the guest of European royalty.

It was on the battlefields of Europe that she decided to organize an American version of the International Red Cross.

She returned to America in 1872 and began work immediately on creating the American Red Cross. She also lent her support and influence to seeking United States ratification of the Geneva Agreement.

In 1881 she incorporated the American Red Cross, naming herself as president. In the process, she added what is now known as "The American Amendment," to the Red Cross dictates.

Her amendment called on both the American and International Red Cross organizations to provide relief and service, not only during times of war and not only for soldiers, but to all citizens during states of natural disasters in wartime or in peace.

A year later, President Chester Arthur signed the Geneva Agreement on behalf of the United States.

For the next 23 years, Clara Barton devoted her life to the Red Cross, traveling to disaster sites throughout America and Europe to provide aid and comfort.

In 1889 she went to Johnstown, Pennsylvania, to help the citizens recover from the devastating Johnstown Flood. In

1891 she traveled to Russia to provide food and care during that country's widespread famine. In 1896 she went to Turkey to provide relief following the Armenian massacre.

At the age of seventy-five she traveled to Cuba to assist American troops and Cuban insurgents during the Spanish American War.

At the age of eighty she traveled to Galveston, Texas, to organize relief efforts for the victims of the Galveston Flood.

In 1902, she traveled to St. Petersburg, Russia, to represent the United States at the Convention of the International Red Cross. Czar Nicholas, presiding at the Convention, bestowed on her the Russian Decoration of the Order of the Red Cross.

She retired from her duties as president of the Red Cross at the age of eighty-three and settled in Glen Echo, Maryland, where she lived out the rest of her life.

On Good Friday, April 12, 1912, at the age of ninety-one she died of natural causes. Her funeral services were held in her hometown of Oxford, Massachusetts, and she was buried in the Oxford Cemetery.

The woman who was born on Christmas Day, 1821, and died on Good Friday, 1912, had devoted more than half her life to providing relief to others throughout the world.

Her obituary, appearing in the *New York Times,* read in part, "She is known wherever man appreciates humanity."

Suggested Reading

Bains, Rae. *Clara Barton: Angel of the Battlefield* (1982).
Grant, Matthew. *Clara Barton: Red Cross Pioneer* (1974).
Hamilton, Leni. *Clara Barton* (1988).
Kent, Zachary. *The Story of Clara Barton* (1987).
Rose, Mary. *Clara Barton: Soldier of Mercy* (1960).

10 WITCH OF WALL STREET
Hetty Green, 1834–1916

"When I was five years old I used to sit on my father's lap while he read the business news and stock market reports of the day to me."

PEOPLE, PLACES AND EVENTS: Hetty Green was unique in American financial affairs, for two reasons. The first was that she made her vast fortune on Wall Street, investing in stocks and bonds, and was knowledgeable enough to prosper during several stock market crashes. The second was that, unlike many women who made fortunes in American business, she gave nothing to charities or philanthropic causes.

The New York Stock Exchange was founded in 1792, organized at the Merchants Coffee House in New York City. It received its official name in 1863, and is the largest securities market in the United States, located at Broad and Wall Streets in the financial district.

Over the years the stock market has experienced a series of panics and crashes, the most devastating one occurring in 1929, which presaged the Great Depression of the 1930s.

During her lifetime, Hetty Green was involved in two market panics, both of which she managed to weather and ultimately prosper from.

The first occurred on "Black Friday," in 1869, when two gold speculators, Jay Gould and James Fish, attempted to corner the gold market in the country. Gould and Fisk tried to dissuade President Ulysses S. Grant from selling government gold. After assuring the gold traders that they had been successful, President Grant put $4 million in government gold up for sale, driving the gold price dramatically down.

The next financial crisis that Green survived was the Panic of 1907 when a sudden drop in the stock market preceded a bank run.

The Panic was caused by over-speculation and unregulated banking and credit lending. Because of the Panic of 1907, Congress passed the Aldrich-Vreeland Act, setting up a commission to oversee the banking and credit industry.

* * * * *

When she died in 1916, Hetty Green left nothing of her approximately $150 million estate to charity. She contributed nothing to charity when she lived, so no one expected otherwise from the woman many newspapers throughout the country called "the richest and most detested woman in America."

Instead, she left everything to her only son, "Colonel" Ned Green, a hugely fat, one-legged eccentric, who proceeded to spent his inheritance on wine, women, lavish parties, yachts and politics. But even he, spending what was estimated at $3 million a year on his pastimes, could not begin to deplete his mother's vast fortune.

"The Colonel," a title in name only, awarded to him by a Southern governor and friend, built a $4 million, 60-room stone and marble mansion overlooking Buzzards Bay in Dartmouth, Massachusetts, on a 300-acre tract of land known as Round Hill, where he lavishly entertained everyone from royalty to prostitutes.

After his death, the mansion was donated to the Massachusetts Institute of Technology.

The Colonel's vices and free-wheeling spending practices were in sharp contrast to his mother Hetty's miserly lifestyle.

Hetty appeared in public in shabby clothes, carried odd bits of food around with her, haggled with shopkeepers over petty purchases, sought medical treatment at charity clinics, and lived in run-down boarding houses. And yet, she was once the richest woman in America and one of the most feared speculators on Wall Street.

A *New York Tribune* reporter described her as wearing "... what once had been a black dress, which must have been made of practically indestructible material. It turned brown, then green and still she wore it; and carried an old umbrella and handbag of about the same era as the dress."

"The Witch of Wall Street," as she became known, was born in New Bedford, Massachusetts, in 1834. Her mother, Abby Howland, inherited a fortune from her father, Isaac Howland, Jr. The Howlands made their fortune in the whaling and merchant shipping business.

Hetty's father, Providence-born Edward Mott Robinson, nicknamed "Black Hawk," after a wily native American chief, ran the Howland family business after the death of Abby's father. He more than tripled the Howland fortune through investments in the stock market.

Always more attached to her father than to her bed-ridden mother, Hetty learned early the importance of a good business mind from her father.

"When I was five years old I used to sit on my father's lap while he read the business news and stock market reports of the day to me," she said. "When I was six I read them myself. And I understood them too."

Brought up as a Quaker, she was educated first at the Quaker Friend's School on Cape Cod and later at James Lowell's School in Boston, run for the daughters of the wealthy New England elite.

At sixteen she was described in New York newspaper society pages as a "vivacious, handsome girl of stately carriage and beautiful hair."

When her father moved his business concerns from New Bedford to New York City, Hetty went with him to help manage his financial affairs.

Black Hawk Robinson, realizing that kerosene, not whale oil, was the wave of the future, sold his interest in the family business for $5 million. The Howland Company had been in business for approximately eighty years. Two years after he sold out, the Howland Company was liquidated.

Hetty began building her fortune shortly after her mother died in 1860. Abby Robinson died without leaving a will. Although Hetty believed she was entitled to all of her mother's money, she allowed her father to decide how the fortune would be distributed. Her father kept the bulk of his wife's fortune, giving Hetty a mere $10,000 in real estate.

It was not until her father died that Hetty truly came into her financial own. Black Hawk Robinson left his entire $6 million fortune to Hetty when he died in June 1865. Shortly after that, Hetty's spinster aunt, Sylvia Ann Howland, died. It was her death and Hetty's subsequent legal actions to gain control of her aunt's fortune that set off what the *Boston Globe* called, "One of the most remarkable will cases in the history of legal jurisprudence."

Her aunt had drawn a will dividing much of her fortune among surviving Howland family members and her favorite charities. She left Hetty a yearly stipend of $70,000. But

Hetty laid claim to her aunt's entire fortune by producing what she claimed was a second will drawn up on her aunt's deathbed.

Already a multi-millionaire five months after her aunt's death, Hetty filed suit in court to secure her aunt's entire fortune, estimated at more than $2 million. The Howland will case dragged on for five years.

Her chief adviser during the case was Edward H. Green. Green, who was fourteen years older than she, had made a small fortune on Wall Street.

The second will produced by Hetty was written entirely in Hetty's own handwriting but ostensibly signed in two places by her aunt. The second will left her aunt's entire fortune to Hetty as "sole heir-at-law."

Although Hetty admitted that the second will was written by her, she claimed it was signed by her aunt. Attorneys for other Howland family members and charities that Sylvia Ann Howland named in her first will declared that the signatures were forged.

Handwriting experts, including the noted Harvard University professor, Dr. Oliver Wendell Holmes, testified that the signatures on the second will presented by Hetty were crudely traced forgeries.

At the height of this controversial case, at age thirty-three, Hetty married her financial adviser, forty-six-year-old Edward Henry Green from Bellow Falls, Vermont. Green was himself a millionaire but his holdings were no match for his wife's financial assets.

When Howland family members, anxious to get their hands on Sylvia Ann Howland's fortune, began discussing ways to bring Hetty to criminal court on charges of forgery, Hetty and her husband fled to London, where they stayed for eight years.

In 1870 the court dismissed Hetty's claim for her aunt's fortune on the grounds of insufficient evidence of a contract between Hetty and her aunt, regardless of what the second will implied. The issue of the forged signatures was never pursued in the courts.

While in London, she had two children: a son, Edward Henry, born in 1868, and a daughter, Sylvia Ann, born in 1871. During this short period in London Hetty spent her time focusing on domestic affairs rather than on finances. It was one of the few times in her life that she ever did.

After moving back to America in 1875, she once again took up the obsessive management of her fortune. She became a major and feared operator on Wall Street.

She held extensive holdings in railroad stocks and government bonds and she maintained considerable liquid assets that she used for lending. She owned more than 8,000 parcels of real estate in the cities of New York, Chicago, St. Louis, Kansas and San Francisco.

She gained much of her fortune following the Panic of 1907. Because she had so much cash at her fingertips, she was able to loan money out to other financiers at an interest rate of six percent, very high in those days.

The Panic of 1907 began with a large drop in the stock market in March, followed by a bank run in October, which caused financial panic everywhere. Caused by over-speculation and unregulated banking and credit lending, the panic resulted in the passage of the Aldrich-Vreeland Act, which levied taxes on securities and established a commission to investigate the banking and credit industry.

Following the Panic of 1907, a great number of Wall Street investors found themselves in Hetty's debt and her fortune increased substantially.

Despite her great wealth, she maintained simplicity in her attire and lifestyle. She hated laziness and waste, and was blunt when dealing with business associates and the public in general.

When a young reporter asked her the reason for her simple lifestyle, she said, "Young man, I am a Quaker."

While living in New York, she was a daily sight, walking in her shabby dress around the financial district of Wall Street.

A *New York Tribune* newspaper article described her frugality by noting that she often carried food in her handbag.

"In Mrs. Green's handbag, she carried graham crackers—bought in bulk—on which she munched from time to time, remarking she was thus saved from paying the prohibitive prices of New York restaurants," the article noted.

Her single-minded devotion to attaining great wealth cost her family dearly— both her husband and her son.

When her husband went bankrupt in 1885, following some ill-advised investments, Hetty refused to underwrite his losses. They separated shortly afterward.

She continued to live with her son and daughter in inexpensive lodgings in New York and New Jersey, avoiding any display of wealth and shunning most of society.

Her eccentricities made her the topic of numerous gossip columns across the country. When her young son's leg became infected following an accident, she refused to hire a physician to tend to it. Instead, with her injured son in tow, she made the rounds of every free medical clinic in Manhattan and Brooklyn.

She was turned away from every clinic she visited. Her reputation as a miser had preceded her. Only then did she turn to a private physician for advice. He advised her that her son's leg needed immediate amputation, but Hetty refused to listen, not based on his medical advice, but on the cost of the operation—$5,000.

Instead, she insisted on treating her son's badly injured leg with home remedies, including massive doses of Carter's Little Liver Pills, and bandages made out of tobacco leaves.

In 1888 Ned Green fell down a flight of stairs while visiting his father, reinjuring his leg. When the doctors were called, they recommended immediate surgery. Gangrene had set in and if the leg wasn't amputated immediately, the infection would soon claim the boy's life.

Ned's father, already bankrupt, sold his few remaining securities to pay for the operation, rather than ask Hetty for the money. Ned's infected right leg was amputated seven inches above the knee at New York City Hospital.

"It's too bad something wasn't done sooner to take care of the leg," the attending physician said.

Ned's leg was buried in the Green Family plot at Immanuel Church in Bellow Falls, Vermont. Forty-seven years later, when Ned died, the leg was exhumed and buried along with the rest of his remains in the family plot.

When her husband passed away in 1902, Hetty attended the funeral in Bellow Falls, accompanied by two of her Wall Street financial advisers. Following the services, she was reported to have remarked, "Well, gentlemen, don't you think we have wasted enough time? Let's get down to business."

Besides her eccentric dress and behavior, in later life she developed a deep paranoia and began carrying a revolver around with her. When asked by a reporter why she had taken out a permit to carry a gun, she said, "Mostly to protect myself against lawyers."

She drew up her own will in 1908, leaving her fortune, estimated at more than $150 million, to her one-legged son and her daughter, Sylvia Ann.

The richest woman in America died alone in a small apartment in Hoboken, New Jersey, eight years later at the age of eighty-one.

She had managed her money with a single-minded purpose—to make more money—and she devoted her life to increasing her fortune, avoiding taxes and ignoring charity.

She was buried at the family cemetery in Bellow Falls.

Few mourned her passing, and the national news media were especially vitriolic in their accounts of her.

"Hetty Green, who lived as a poor woman lives, and moved from one place to another to dodge those pestering her with appeals for aid, was unable to take her immense fortune with her when she quit this world for the next," read the account in the *Boston Transcript*.

Following the death of her son in 1936 at the age of sixty-seven, the entire family fortune passed into the hands of Hetty's only daughter, Sylvia Ann. When she died in 1951 at the age of eighty, Hetty's fortune was finally distributed, much of it going to taxes and the rest amongst Howland family heirs, who little needed it.

"The wealth from which Hetty Green and her tall, austere, lonely daughter derived so little pleasure, aside from the satisfaction of possessing it and watching it grow, was originally, in the words of Herman Melville, dredged up from the depths of the ocean," the *New Bedford Standard Times* said following Sylvia Ann's death.

Hetty Green, the "Witch of Wall Street," lost her fortune to time, death and progress— everything she despised.

Suggested Reading

Clark, William. *The Robber Baroness* (1979).
Emery, William. *The Howland Heirs* (1919).
Lewis, Arthur. *The Day They Shook the Plum Tree* (1963).
Robinson, Richard. *United States Business History 1602–1988* (1990).
Sparkes, Boyden. *The Witch Of Wall Street: Hetty Green* (1936).

11 MOTHER OF INVENTIONS
Margaret Knight, 1838–1914

"I'm only sorry I couldn't have had as good a chance as a boy and have been put to my trade regularly."

PEOPLE, PLACES AND EVENTS: The first patent awarded to an American was issued in 1641 by the British to Samuel Winslow of Massachusetts for a salt-processing invention.

The first woman in America to be awarded a patent by the U.S. Patent Office was a New Englander, Mary Kies of Connecticut, who was awarded a patent in 1809 for the invention of a weaving process.

Between 1800 and 1900, more than 8,000 patents were issued to women inventors.

The U.S. Patent Office was not established until 1790, and the first American to receive a U.S. patent that year was Samuel Hopkins of Vermont, for his potash-making process.

U.S. Patent Office records show that more inventors come from New England than any other region of the country, and traditionally most patents are issued to people living in Connecticut.

One of the first woman inventors was Amanda Jones (1835–1914) from New York. In 1873 she was granted several patents for her food-processing inventions.

In 1880 she patented a fuel burner used in furnaces and boilers. From 1903 to 1914, she was awarded seven new patents on her food-processing and fuel-burner inventions.

In 1890 in Chicago, she began her own food processing company, The Woman's Canning and Preserving Company. Nearly all of the company's employees and stockholders were women.

* * * * *

Margaret Knight was not the first woman to be awarded a United States patent, although she was no doubt the most prolific American woman inventor, holding twenty-seven patents at the time of her death.

When she died in 1914 at the age of seventy-six, an obituary in the *Framingham News* in Massachusetts called Margaret Knight "A woman Thomas Edison."

Given that she had no real formal education beyond grade school, her achievements are startling. What is more remarkable than the number of inventions to her credit is that so many of them had to do with heavy machinery.

Even though she was unaware of the scientific and mechanical principles behind many of her inventions, she had the ability to grasp a mechanical concept, and visualize the machinery she wanted to build to solve a problem or better an existing machine.

Margaret Knight was born in York, Maine, in 1838, and spent much of her childhood there and in Manchester, New Hampshire. Even as a young girl, she demonstrated an uncanny ability with tools.

"As a child I never cared for the things that girls usually do; dolls never had any charms for me," she wrote a friend in later years.

"I couldn't see the sense of coddling bits of porcelain with faces; the only things I wanted were a jackknife, a gimlet and a piece of wood. My friends were horrified."

"I was always making things for my brothers ... . I was famous for my kites, and my sleds were the envy and admiration of all the boys in town," she wrote.

Tall and gangly, she had a youthful appearance even in later life and a soft voice.

Her family moved from Maine to New Hampshire while she was still a child. It was in Manchester, at the age of twelve, that she created her first invention—a safety device for a powered textile loom.

She and her brothers had gone to work in what was once the Amoskeag Manufacturing Company, a textile mill, in Manchester. Her first invention came about while watching the shuttles of one of the massive textile looms in the mill.

When one of the shuttles accidently became unhinged and flew out of joint, injuring a mill worker, she had the idea of inventing a locking device that would shut down the shuttle when accidents occurred. Her invention, she imagined, would prevent further dangerous accidents.

It took her six months to perfect her invention. At first, despite a successful demonstration of the device, the mill owners were reluctant to apply her invention to their textile process. She met with such resistance throughout her life.

Long after she was recognized as an accomplished inventor, with several dozen patents to her name, she still often encountered skepticism from manufacturers. Even the laborers hired to build the machines she designed questioned her ability to oversee the production of her own inventions, despite the fact that she had written all the plans and specifications.

She remained persistent in every confrontation, however, and ultimately she was able to gain the respect of mill owners and workmen for her competency. Her first invention, the stop-motion lock for the textile loom, was finally adopted at the mill where she worked.

Despite her early success, it was not until 1870, at the age of thirty-two, that she applied for and received her first patent. This too was a struggle.

Up until this time, she had not thought to apply for a patent for any of her inventions, but in 1870, when someone attempted to steal one, it became necessary to fight for patents on her work.

In 1867, while working at a small company in Springfield, Massachusetts, that manufactured paper bags, she came up with an idea for a machine that would create square-bottomed paper bags. Until her invention, bags were flat-ended, like grain bags. Her invention would revolutionize the paper bag industry.

The invention she came up with is still being used today to manufacture paper bags like ones used in supermarkets.

After first conceiving of the machine, she built what she called "a guide finger and plate knife folder," used to construct the square bottom of the bags. She attached the device to one of the existing bag machines at the Springfield shop where she was working and successfully produced the first square-bottomed paper bag.

Her next step was to build a full-scale wooden model of the machine, and she drew up the plans and specifications for it herself. Finally, she had a working cast-iron version of the new machine built.

It was constructed in Boston and she went there often to work on improvements and oversee its construction. It was during this time that she allowed another inventor, Charles Annan, to see her device. Subsequently, Annan designed, built and applied for his own patent on a similar machine.

During the course of the three years Knight took perfecting her machine, she did not apply for a patent. When she finally did, Annan sued to stop her, claiming that he had created his machine first.

In 1870, the Commissioner of Patents at the U.S. Patent Office in Washington, D. C., decided that, based on documents presented by Knight, she had conceived of the machine well before Annan did his work. The Commissioner awarded Knight the patent for her new machine.

In making his decision, the Commissioner pointed out that Knight had "little practical acquaintance with machinery," so he could therefore overlook her delay in applying for the patent.

The confrontation with Annan taught her a valuable lesson about filing for patents and about revealing her inventions to others. After that she seldom developed any device of importance without patenting it.

Knight was not bothered by the apprehensiveness she encountered from men about her many inventions. Noting that as a child she was called a tomboy, she said, "That made very little impression on me. I sighed sometimes because I was not like other girls, but wisely concluded that I couldn't help it and sought further consolation from my tools."

Not all of her inventions were related to heavy machinery and manufacturing. After moving to Ashland, Massachusetts, she invented a dress and skirt shield in 1883, a robe clasp in 1884 and a cooking spit for fireplaces in 1885. In 1894 she patented a revolutionary new window and sash for use in homes.

In the 1890s she moved her base of operations to Framingham, Massachusetts, where she lived the rest of her life, while maintaining a small workshop in Boston.

Following her move to Framingham, she devoted herself to inventing machines used in the manufacture of shoes.

During this period, she was granted six separate patents for a variety of shoe-cutting machines.

Toward the end of her life, she worked on a variety of inventions for improving rotary engines and motors. She received her first patent on her automotive designs in 1902 and was awarded her last in 1915, a year after her death.

Part of her work involved the design and development of a sleeve valve for a rotary engine that she presented to the Knight-Davidson Motor Company in New York. Although it was unique in design, the car company turned it down.

None of the many inventions she created brought her wealth. It had been her practice over the years to sell her inventions outright to various employers, and so she received no royalties on her inventions. She was once offered royalties for one of her inventions that would have earned her $50,000, but she sold it outright for $500.

As an inventor she was never interested in the development of scientific theory as it applied to her many inventions. Her primary concern was focused on the practical application of the devices she conceived and built.

"I am not surprised at what I've done," she wrote to a friend. "I'm only sorry I couldn't have had as good a chance as a boy and have been put to my trade regularly."

She died at Framingham Hospital in 1914 and was buried in Newton Cemetery.

Suggested Reading

De Camp, L. S. *The Heroic Age of American Inventions* (1961).
Fuller, Edmund. *Tinkers and Genius* (1955).
Hylander, Clarence. *American Inventors* (1960).
James, Edward. *Notable American Women 1607–1950*.
Kaempfferty, Waldeman. *A Popular History of American Inventions* (1924).

12 KEEPER OF THE LIGHT
Ida Lewis, 1842–1911

"The light is my child and I know when it needs me, even when I sleep."

PEOPLE, PLACES AND EVENTS: The first lighthouse in America was built in 1716 in the Massachusetts Bat Colony, erected on Little Brewster Island in Boston Harbor.

The first lighthouse on the Pacific coast was built on Point Loma, in San Diego, California.

Ida Lewis, America's foremost lifesaver, made her first daring rescue at sea in 1858 when she was sixteen years old. She made her last rescue in 1906 when she was sixty-five.

The population of the country in 1858 was an estimated 31 million people. By the turn of the century it had grown to more than 75 million.

In 1858, when Lewis made her first sea rescue, James Buchanan (1791–1868) was President and the country was on the verge of the Civil War.

The first horse-drawn trolleys were introduced in Philadelphia and the first Atlantic cable message was sent from Queen Victoria to President Buchanan. In New York, more than 1,500 people paid fifty cents each to watch the New York All Stars beat Brooklyn by a score of 22 to 18—the first paid admission to a baseball game.

By 1906, the year Lewis made her last rescue, Theodore Roosevelt (1858–1919) was President. Orville Wright had flown for twelve seconds and 120 feet at Kitty Hawk, North Carolina, and radio enthusiast Reginald Fessenden of Massachusetts had made the first radio broadcast.

San Francisco was hit by an earthquake that caused more than $350 million in damage, and President Roosevelt sent the first around-the-world cable message in a matter of twelve minutes.

The first World Series was held in 1903, with the American League Boston Red Sox, known as the Red Stockings, beating the National League Pittsburgh Pirates, five games to three.

*****

In the winter of 1906, when sixty-five-year-old Ida Lewis rowed out into Narragansett Bay in a raging gale to save a woman whose boat had capsized, it was the last but not the first time she had saved someone from a watery grave.

Miss Lewis was the heroine of eighteen daring rescues at sea during her nearly fifty years as the keeper of the light at the Lime Rock Lighthouse in Newport, Rhode Island. Her record as a lifesaver far surpassed that of Grace Darling, the English lighthouse keeper who saved five people during her career. It is a record that still stands.

Born in Newport in 1842, she went to the Lime Rock Lighthouse with her father, Capt. Hosea Lewis, when he was appointed keeper of the light by the Federal Lighthouse Service.

The lighthouse stood in Newport Harbor on a rocky ledge overlooking Narragansett Bay. The beacon could be seen far out to sea, across Narragansett Bay, all the way to the military fortress, Fort Adams.

She and her mother, father and three brothers and sisters all lived in the small, whitewashed, two-story house attached to the lighthouse.

"All the sea, all the sky, all the joy of the great free world and plenty of room to enjoy it," Lewis said of her lighthouse home.

Along with her other chores at the lighthouse, every morning she rowed her brothers and sisters to the mainland school in Newport and returned again in the evening to row them back.

She quickly came to know every rock and shoal in the dangerous bay and was able to memorize safe passages across the currents.

When her father suffered a paralyzing stroke, she gradually assumed his duties as keeper of the light.

In 1858, when she was only sixteen, she rowed out and pulled four fishermen to safety whose boat had capsized. It was the start of what would become the most illustrious career of any American woman lifesaver.

In 1866, she saved a half-drowned sailor who had fallen overboard from his skiff.

And in 1867, she saved three Irish sheepherders who were transporting several prize sheep across the bay. After saving the three men, she rowed back out and rescued the sheep.

"Whenever I see your light shining, I'll put up a prayer for its keeper. And if my new baby is a girl, she'll be named Ida Lewis," one of the thankful sheepherders said as he huddled in front of the fire at Lewis' Lime Rock home.

She would fly across the waves in her small skiff, at any time of day or night, in any kind of weather, at the slightest sight of any speck on the distant water which her well-trained eye recognized as a person in distress.

On two occasions in a single year, the young girl rescued three people stranded far out on the frozen waves of the wintry harbor. Many times, she helped weathered sea captains navigate their ships safely through the bay in dense fog.

Sea captains and Fort Adams soldiers alike all came to know and respect the young girl for her bravery and knowledge of the sea.

"In danger, look for the dark-haired girl in a rowboat and follow her," was the word that spread up and down the Rhode Island coast and beyond.

But, it was not until 1869 that she won national recognition for her many feats of bravery.

In a howling blizzard, two soldiers rowing across the bay to their station at Fort Adams capsized their boat. They were barely clinging to life when Lewis, barefoot and without a coat, rowed through frigid wind and snow to rescue them.

The soldiers were unconscious and clinging to the keel of their boat when she pulled them to safety. She rowed them back to Lime Rock where she restored their breathing.

A *New York Times* reporter staying in Newport heard of the daring rescue and filed a story with his paper about her exploits.

Instantly, she became known from New England to California.

A *Harper's Magazine* article published in June, 1869, described her as a "slender, blue-eyed girl, with light brown hair, frank and hearty."

The author of the article pondered in print whether it was "feminine" for women to row boats, but then concluded that "None but a donkey would consider it unfeminine to save lives."

"Anyone would rescue a drowning man, of course. I just happen to be where I see them first," Lewis said.

Susan B. Anthony, the leader of the suffrage movement in America, hailed her exploits as further evidence of women's broad competency in any field of endeavor.

Things happened quickly following the series of newspaper and magazine articles.

In July 1869 the people of Newport presented her with a new lifeboat, "The Rescue," in recognition of her many acts of bravery.

The soldiers at Fort Adams showed their appreciation by giving her a gold watch and chain.

Even General Ulysses S. Grant (1822–1885) participated in the testimonial to her, sending along a message proclaiming the Lime Rock Lighthouse as "The Ida Lewis Light."

Along with the many accolades, she received hundreds of marriage proposals from men around the country. It was all daunting for the quiet, reserved lighthouse keeper.

Ultimately, she accepted the proposal of William Wilson, a Connecticut sailor and fisherman, and in 1870 they were married in a small ceremony in Newport.

The marriage didn't last long. Wilson wanted her to move back to the mainland with him but she was wedded to the lighthouse and would not leave.

Although she did not believe in divorce, she did believe in separation. She remained at the lighthouse when her husband left and continued to be known as Miss Lewis.

When her father passed away in 1872, she was left as the sole caretaker of the lighthouse. She continued to live on her island home with her younger brother Rudolph, her dog and six cats.

In 1879, the Federal Government finally recognized her and made her the official keeper of the light. She was the first woman ever appointed to such a position by the Federal Lighthouse Service.

Over the course of the next twenty years she remained steadfast in her job, guiding ships through the treacherous harbor, rescuing hapless sailors, doing her job with courage, pride and zeal.

In 1906, she saved her eighteenth person. She was awarded a gold American Cross of Honor medal by Congress and became a lifetime beneficiary of the Carnegie Hero Fund, which awarded her a monthly pension of thirty dollars.

These were added to the hundreds of other awards and recognitions that adorned her small home at the lighthouse.

But by the turn of the century things had begun to change in the Federal Lighthouse Service. After nearly fifty years, she began receiving unfavorable reports from the Washington offices. One report indicated that she was "not following the new order of things."

Following this came a report in the local newspaper that the government was contemplating closing the Lime Rock Lighthouse in favor of a full-fledged Coast Guard station.

The reports sent her into a fit of depression. Her health began to fail.

In October 1911, while alone tending to the lighthouse, she suffered a stroke. Her brother found her unconscious on the floor.

Since there was no telephone connection, he had to row to the mainland to get a doctor.

Word of her stroke spread quickly along the Rhode Island coast. Rowboats, fishing vessels, pleasure crafts and sailboats all lined up in the harbor for a candlelight vigil in her honor.

The Fall River liner "The Priscilla," passing on its way from Newport to New York, tolled its bells on board in honor the stricken lighthouse heroine.

"The light is my child and I know when it needs me, even when I sleep. This is home to me and I hope the good Lord will take me away when I have to leave it," she had once said.

Ida Lewis died without regaining consciousness on Oct. 24, 1911, where she had lived all her life, at the Lime Rock Lighthouse.

The keeper of the light had gone out forever. She was buried in the Common Ground on Farewell Street in Newport. After her death, the Lime Rock Lighthouse was also closed forever.

Suggested Reading

Beaver, Patrick. *A History of Lighthouses* (1971).
Gleason, Sarah. *Kindly Lights* (1991).
Muir, Charles. *Women the Makers of History* (1956).
Riley, Glenda. *Inventing the American Woman* (1987).
Uglow, Jennifer, ed. *The Continuum Dictionary of Women's Biography* (1989).

13 PURPLE MOUNTAINS' MAJESTY
Annie Peck, 1850–1932

"I am here at last, after all these years, but shall we ever get down?"

PEOPLE, PLACES AND EVENTS: Women adventurers like Annie Peck abounded in American society, dating as far back as 1704, when Sarah Knight (1666–1727) set off from her home in Boston alone, on horseback, riding to New Haven, Connecticut, and then to New York City.

A journey of this length, undertaken by a woman alone, was unheard of during this period.

Knight kept a detailed journal during her three-month trek in which she dutifully recorded the food she ate, the sights she saw, the places she stayed, the people she met and the customs she encountered.

In 1825, nearly 100 years after her death, her journal was published as *The Journal of Madam Knight*. The book became an instant success and a valuable historical document detailing the life and times of Colonial America.

Explorer Osa Johnson (1894–1953), from Kansas, made her reputation as an early wildlife filmmaker.

She and her husband traveled to the Solomon Islands, Borneo and Africa, filming live action accounts of the exotic environment and wildlife.

Their first film, "Jungle Adventures," appeared in 1921, followed in 1922 by "Head Hunters of the South Seas."

Their films were immediate commercial successes.

Eliza Scidmore (1856–1928) set out alone to explore Alaska. Her book, *Alaska, Its Southern Coast and the Sitkan Archipelago,* was published in 1885.

As a member of the National Geographic Society, she traveled extensively in China and Japan, and many of her articles appeared in *National Geographic* magazine, accompanied by photographs she had taken herself.

But of all the many American women explorers, none was more intertwined with the life and times of mountain climber Annie Peck than Fanny Workman (1859–1925), born in Worcester, Massachusetts.

In 1899, Workman and her husband, William, a retired physician, made their first of seven expeditions through the largely unexplored Karakorum mountain range of the Himalayas. They returned to explore the Himalayas in 1902, 1903, 1906, 1908, 1911 and 1912.

In 1903, Workman climbed Koser Gunga, a 21,000-foot peak, setting a world record for women mountain climbers.

In 1906, she successfully scaled the 23,000-foot peak of Nun Hun, setting another mountain climbing world altitude record for women.

When Annie Peck made her record-setting climb of 24,000 feet to the peak of South America's Mount Huascaran, Workman employed a group of engineers to disprove Peck's claim.

*****

Annie Peck, America's foremost woman mountain climber, was eighty-two years old when she climbed Mount Madison in New Hampshire, an ascent of 5,380 feet. It was her last climb; she died three years later.

Born in Providence, Rhode Island, in 1850, she made her first successful climb in 1888 when she scaled Mount Shasta (14,380 feet) in California. This was followed by a series of record-shattering climbs that catapulted her into worldwide fame.

A teacher of the classics, her obsession with the rigors of mountain climbing came to her late in life.

In 1883, she became the first woman admitted to the American School of Classical Studies in Athens, Greece. It was there, while touring in Europe, that she had her first glimpse of the Matterhorn. The sight of the nearly 15,000-foot mountain stirred in her a driving interest in climbing.

"No one is acquainted with mountains who sees them only from valleys or from railroad trains. The wide expanse of earth and heaven, the stillness, calm and peace there should attract and charm every soul with a love of beauty," she said.

In 1895, dressed in what would become her signature attire—boots, knickers, tunic and a floppy hat tied onto her head with a heavy scarf—she became the first woman ever to climb the Matterhorn, which made her an instant celebrity.

"I felt I should never be happy until I too should scale those frowning walls," she said of her Matterhorn ascent.

She was the most unlikely of mountain climbers. A teacher, and older than many climbers of her day, she often surprised people when they met her in person. She was slight of frame and feminine in appearance. But she had remarkable physical strength and endurance.

Her father, George Peck, was a prominent Providence lawyer. Her mother, Ann, was a direct descendant of Roger Williams, the founder of Rhode Island.

Although both parents were opposed to her climbing adventures, her brothers supported her efforts.

She had grown up constantly competing with her older brothers and attributed to this sibling competition the development of her physical stamina and fearlessness.

An outspoken women's rights advocate, this too she admitted was a natural outgrowth of her insistence on equal status with her brothers.

In 1911, when she was sixty-one years old, she became the first person to scale 21,250-foot Mount Coropuna in Peru, where she planted a flag bearing the words "Votes for Women," at the peak.

She attended Dr. Stockbridge's School for Young Ladies in Providence and Providence High School, and graduated from the Rhode Island State Normal School (Rhode Island College) in 1872.

After teaching for two years in Providence public schools, she enrolled at the University of Michigan, which offered equal education for men and women. She majored in Greek and graduated in 1878.

From 1881 until 1883, she taught Latin at Purdue University and later taught at Smith College.

She gave parlor lectures on Greek and Roman archaeology to raise money to travel. By 1892, lecturing was her sole source of income.

In 1897, backed financially by the *New York World* newspaper, which had a history of sponsoring women, she climbed 18,700-foot Mount Orizaba in Mexico, the highest point ever reached by a woman.

"I felt that any great achievement would be an advantage to my sex," she said.

In 1906 she began her quest to climb the peak of Mount Huascaran in Peru. At an estimated height of nearly 24,000 feet, it was the highest peak any woman would have ever reached.

She was unsuccessful in her first two attempts. Always underfunded for her mountain climbing expeditions, she often lacked accurate data on the mountain terrain, as well as proper clothing and gear. Her porters were usually inexperienced, and because she was a woman they were unwilling to follow her orders and judgment when it came to the treacherous climbs.

Her own desire to succeed far overshadowed any concern for her personal safety, dangers and sickness, and she had no patience for those who did not share her climbing obsession, no matter what the cost.

In 1908, still poorly funded and equipped, she and two guides undertook a third expedition to the summit of Mount Huascaran. High winds and frigid cold made the ascent nearly impossible, but still they continued upward.

Finally Peck and her two guides made it to the summit.

"I am here at last, after all these years, but shall we ever get down?" she said.

The intrepid band of climbers nearly didn't make it back down. The wind and the cold made the climbing surface a sheet of glass. Although they did make it back safely, one of her guides suffered frostbite and his foot and part of one of his hands had to be amputated. Annie Peck was unscathed.

She became an international celebrity after the climb. The President of Peru awarded her a gold medal and the North Peak of Huascaran was renamed "Ana Peck," in her honor.

The ascent was later accurately measured at 22,000 feet. Although her climb did not smash the world record for height, she still had climbed higher than any man or woman in the Western Hemisphere.

Along with founding the American Alpine Club, she was the author of several books, including *A Search for the Apex of South America,* published in 1911. The book was a chronicle of her many near disasters climbing mountains.

Following her last climb in 1932 at eighty-two, she devoted the remainder of her life to traveling abroad.

Her last visit was to Athens, Greece. She died in 1935 in a New York City hotel room at the age of eighty-five. Her body was cremated and her ashes buried in North Burial Ground in Providence, Rhode island.

Her obituary in the *New York Times* called her "A humanist, who could not leave the world without one more glimpse of the Parthenon."

Suggested Reading

Land, Barbara. *The New Explorers* (1981).
Lauter, Estella. *Women as Mythmakers* (1984).
Messer, Reinhold. *The Big Walls* (1978).
Preston, Wheeler. *American Biographies* (1940).
Smith, George. *Introduction to Mountaineering* (1957).

14 MEASURE FOR MEASURE
Fannie Farmer, 1857–1915

"Good judgment, with experience, has taught some to measure by sight, but the majority need definite guides."

PEOPLE, PLACES AND EVENTS: The first cooking school in America was started in 1877 by Juliet Corson in New York City. Corson, who was born in Roxbury, Massachusetts, taught women how to buy and cook healthy, inexpensive meals.

Her pamphlet, "Fifteen Cent Dinners for Families of Six," became a huge success, as did her school. Like Fannie Farmer, Corson paid for the publication of her cooking pamphlet herself. Over 50,000 copies of the publication were sold within a year of its appearance.

In 1878, she was asked to lecture about nutrition in Washington, D.C., before the Training School for Nurses.

Another cook and author, Irma von Starkloff Rombauer, also achieved tremendous world-wide success with a self-published cookbook. Born in St. Louis, Missouri, in 1877, Rombauer collected some of her favorite recipes and published them herself under the title of *The Joy of Cooking*. The book included basic, self-help instructions on the preparation of food, menu planning and recipes.

By 1975, *The Joy of Cooking*, considered now an indispensable book for any cook's library, had sold nearly nine million copies.

The Boston Cooking School was begun in 1878 by the Women's Education Association of Boston. The first director of the school was Carrie Dearborn. The aim of the school was to teach cooking teachers, rather than household cooks.

One of the first teachers at the school was Mary Bailey Lincoln, who was born in South Attleboro, Massachusetts, and later attended Wheaton College in nearby Norton, Massachusetts.

While teaching at the Boston Cooking School, Lincoln wrote *The Boston Cook Book*, a collection of favorite recipes and cooking instructions. It was published in 1884 and was a huge commercial success.

From 1885 to 1889, Lincoln taught at the Lasell Seminary in Auburndale, Massachusetts. During this time she published three more highly successful cookbooks, and was part owner of *The American Kitchen Magazine*.

* * * * *

It is ironic that the book that taught Americans to cook, *Boston Cooking School Cook Book*, published in 1896, was written by a Bostonian and published first in a city where Puritanical ethics had long taught that eating for pleasure was sinful. The author of this enormously successful book was Fannie Farmer. She is credited with inventing the modern recipe.

Besides writing this all-time, best-selling American cookbook, Farmer's most significant contribution to the art of cooking was the invention of level-spoon measurements, which made all recipes more exact in their preparation.

Before the publication of *Boston Cooking School Cook Book*, cooking ingredients were measured by such arbitrary designations as "a handful" of this, a "pinch" of that, or a "heaping spoonful" of whatever.

Her introduction of uniform and accurate measurements standardized all recipes. After its publication and the popularization of level measurements, cooks throughout the country no longer had to guess about what size egg to use or how big a pinch of salt was required.

Her recipes called for cups and spoons to be filled with whatever ingredient was called for and a knife used to cut off whatever did not fit into the measuring utensil. Using this method, the ingredients fit exactly into the measuring utensil, the top surface always even with the edge of the cup or spoon.

Her creation of level measurements has become as standard to American cooking as the Roman alphabet is to the English language. Her system forever changed American cooking from an arbitrary guessing game to a culinary science.

"Good judgment, with experience, has taught some to measure by sight, but the majority need definite guides.

"Correct measurements are absolutely necessary to obtain the best results. A cupful of liquid is all the cup will hold. A tea or tablespoon is all the spoon will hold," she wrote.

Along with pioneering the use of standard level measurements in cooking, Farmer popularized cooking for the average American family.

Her parents, John and Mary Farmer, planned to send their tall, red-haired daughter to college, but, when she was seventeen years old and a student at Medfield High School, she was stricken with a mysterious paralysis, caused either by a mild stroke or polio.

The paralysis left her crippled and forced to limp for the rest of her life. Socially, the condition made her unacceptable to most suitors.

The family physician discouraged any attempts at further schooling, so she was forced to cancel plans to attend college.

Eventually, she recovered from the paralysis sufficiently to go to work as a housekeeper in the home of a family friend, Mrs. Charles Shaw of Boston.

It was while working in the Shaw household that she developed a keen interest in cooking. While she was employed there, she began to formulate her ideas on standard measurements for recipes.

The idea came to her while caring for Mrs. Shaw's daughter, Marcia, who watched Fannie prepare food for the family and tried to copy her.

Because Marcia was confused by the vague recipe directions, Fannie developed her own system of recipe instructions that made it easy for the young girl to follow.

The standardized recipes and level measurements were born out of Fannie's desire to provide young Marcia Shaw with clear and easy-to-follow instructions when preparing food.

Fannie developed such a keen interest in cooking that her family urged her to enter the Boston Cooking School, run by Carrie Dearborn.

Her parents wanted her to develop her knowledge of cooking at the school in the hopes she would find a calling with which she could support herself. Fannie liked the idea and ultimately enrolled in the school when she was twenty-eight years old.

Her performance at the school was so outstanding that when she graduated from the school in 1889, Mrs. Dearborn asked her to join the staff of the school as assistant director.

Following the death of Mrs. Dearborn in 1891, Fannie became the director of the school.

It was while she was serving as director that she published her famous and monumental cookbook. The cookbook was a plain-looking volume of approximately 600 pages. It sold for a mere $2.00 per copy.

When she first brought her manuscript to a publisher, Little, Brown & Company in Boston, the editors were so nervous about her revolutionary level-measurement recipes that they insisted Fannie pay for the production costs herself.

Little, Brown & Company had so little faith in the potential success of the book that they printed only 3,000 copies of the first edition. Although sales were originally limited to students at the Boston Cooking School, word of the publication spread rapidly, and the book went on to sell more than four million copies.

Publication of the book made Fannie Farmer a household name. Twenty-one editions of the book had been printed by the time of Fannie's death in 1915, making it the sixth best-selling hardcover cookbook in history.

The original book came complete with elaborate directions for building different types of fires to cook with, besides the revolutionary level-measure recipes. The intent of the book was to cover plain, good, home-style cooking. It did not delve into any glamorous gourmet delights.

When originally published, some of the recipes called for wine and brandy. During Prohibition, recipes calling for alcohol were removed from these editions and restored following the repeal of Prohibition.

Throughout her life, Fannie revised and created new recipes that she tested completely before including in her cookbook.

The cookbook was published at a time in America when cooks, either homemakers or professional chefs, could only choose between simple recipe guides, filled with ambiguous measurements and directions, or elaborate books concocted by professional chefs and aimed at families that could afford a professional chef and servants, and who had at their disposal large quantities of cooking supplies and utensils.

Fannie's book was geared to an average American family and offered simple, accurate and comprehensive instructions for cooking. The book provided Americans with a soup-to-nuts cookbook from which anyone could learn to cook.

Most of her recipes were aimed at eating for healthful reasons, rather than simply enjoyment. All her recipes were designed to attain the best, most reliable and delicious tastes.

Fannie's book remains the target of criticism by food critics throughout the world, especially French culinary snobs.

According to Bill Rhode, an editor of *Gourmet Magazine*, Fannie's book "... will teach all the basic things—how to boil and broil and so on. Fannie is a good guide on the foothills but not the mountains," of epicurean delight.

Noted magazine columnist and social critic H. L. Mencken (1880–1956) reviewed the book, saying, "The weaknesses of the work lie in two directions. First, it is written by a woman and addressed to women, and hence a certain tea-table preciosity gets into some of the recipes ... . The other defect of the book apparently flows out of the fact that it was hatched in Boston, where lower middle class British notions of cookery still prevail. Thus it deals very badly with the great dishes of more cultured regions."

Mencken went on to allow that although Fannie's book was geared too much for women and too New England in its temperament, it was still "a very worthy work."

None of this deterred Fannie, nor should it have, since her work has outsold and outlasted any of her critics, including Mencken.

Although she did not address issues like calories, fat and vitamins in her book, she was well aware of these subjects.

"With the progress of knowledge the needs of the human body have not been forgotten," she wrote in the preface to the first edition of the book.

"I certainly feel that the time is not far distant when a knowledge of the principles of diet will be an essential part of one's education. Mankind will eat to live, will be able to do better mental and physical work, and disease will be less frequent."

After serving eleven years as the director of the Boston Cooking School, she resigned and began her own school— Miss Farmer's School of Cookery. The new school was, like her famous cookbook, innovative and revolutionary.

Courses at the Boston Cooking School were aimed at training cooking teachers. Fannie's new school emphasized educating housewives and homemakers. Her goal was to provide education and practice in cooking to people who would actually be doing the cooking in a household.

Along with regular cooking classes at her school, she taught classes in cooking for invalids, and also taught a class on the subject of cooking for invalids at Harvard Medical School. All of her classes were well-attended, with some classes containing 200 students.

She taught twice a week at the school and became a much-sought-after lecturer. For ten years, she also wrote a popular column on cooking for the *Woman's Home Companion*, a national magazine.

In 1907, she suffered a stroke which completely paralyzed her legs. Although her health became worse and her ability to move about was limited, she often lectured to audiences and taught her classes from a wheelchair.

During her life, she also published *Chafing Dish Possibilities* (1898), *Food and Cookery for the Sick and Convalescent* (1904), *What to Have for Dinner* (1905), *Catering for Special Occasions* (1911), and *A New Book of Cookery* (1912).

None of these books, however, were as successful as her first. After her death, succeeding editions of "the book" were edited first by her sister, Cora (Farmer) Perkins, and next by her niece.

Her last public lecture was given in Boston just ten days before her death. She died in Boston in 1915 at the age of fifty-seven and is buried in that city. Her school, Miss Farmer's School of Cookery, lasted for another thirty years, finally closing in 1944.

Suggested Reading

Smallzried, Kathleen. *The Everlasting Pleasure* (1956).
Tierney, Helen. *Women's Studies Encyclopedia* (1990).
Warren, Ruth. *A Pictorial History of Women in America* (1975).
Uglow, Jennifer, ed. *The Continuum of Women's Biography* (1981).
Vare, Ethlie Ann, and Greg Ptacek. *Mothers of Invention* (1988).

15 A SELF-DETERMINED LIFE
Blanche Ames, 1878–1969

"For her to have an idea was to act, no matter how difficult or impossible."

PEOPLE, PLACES AND EVENTS: On the steps of a Cincinnati Courthouse in 1828, Scottish-born Fanny Wright (1795–1852) proclaimed, "Let women stand where they may. Their position decides that of the race!"

Her's was one of the first declaration of women's rights, a fight that culminated nearly 100 years later in the passage of the Nineteenth Amendment to the Constitution, giving women the right to vote.

In 1848, the first organized women's convention was held in Seneca Falls, New York, where a "Declaration of Sentiments" was issued. Modeled after the Declaration of Independence, it called for all women to have "immediate admission to all the rights and privileges which belong to them as citizens of the United States."

The convention was organized by Lucretia Mott (1793–1880) from Nantucket, Massachusetts, and Elizabeth Cady Stanton (1815–1902) from New York.

Neither woman would live to see the day when all American women were granted the right to vote.

In 1869, the National Woman Suffrage Association was founded. Stanton was elected president of the organization. Susan B. Anthony (1820–1906) of Adams, Massachusetts, was one of the driving forces behind the association.

In 1872, Anthony became the first woman in America to cast a vote in a presidential election, when she illegally voted in Rochester, New York. She was arrested, found guilty and fined $100 for her actions.

In 1878, a women's suffrage amendment was introduced into the United States Senate by California Senator Aaron A. Sargent. It was defeated, but the amendment was introduced into every session of Congress over the next forty-two years.

In 1918, at the outbreak of America's involvement in World War I, President Woodrow Wilson told the U.S. Senate that woman's suffrage was a "virtually necessary war measure."

In 1919, Wilson pushed through Congress the Nineteenth Amendment. Within a month, eleven states had ratified the Amendment. In August 1920, the State of Tennessee became the thirty-sixth state to ratify the Amendment, making it law. The ratification came in time for American women to vote freely, for the first time in American history, during the presidential election of 1920.

*****

Blanche Ames danced around the huge table in her family library in Easton, Massachusetts, when the news that Republican United States Senate hopeful, John Wingate Weeks, went down to defeat in the election of 1918.

Her joyful jaunt was not propelled in any way by her partisanship. She and her family were staunch Republicans. Her father-in-law, Oliver Ames, served as a Republican Governor of Massachusetts from 1887 to 1890.

The engine that drove Blanche's victory dance, with her husband Oakes in tow, was the anticipation that a Constitutional amendment giving women the right to vote was now one vote closer to being adopted.

Elected in Week's place was David Walsh, only the fourth Democrat to be elected to that office and the state's first Catholic. Besides being a Democrat in a predominantly Republican State, and a Catholic to boot, Walsh was one very important thing to Blanche Ames. He was a suffragist.

She had devoted five years of her life, beginning in 1913, to the suffragist movement. Organizing against Weeks and helping to defeat him was one step in the long road to getting women the vote.

The political death knell for Weeks came when he told a delegation of suffragists at the Massachusetts Constitutional Convention of 1917 that he would not vote for the suffrage amendment, "even if the whole State of Massachusetts urged me to do so."

The whole state wouldn't. In fact, delegates at the 1917 Constitutional Convention defeated a suffragist amendment. But, the strong-willed Blanche Ames was asking Weeks to support the movement. When he declined, she, despite her and her family's long-time Republican party affiliation, set out to defeat him. And she did.

Blanche's involvement in the suffragist movement and in Week's defeat caused division in the large, socially prominent Ames family. Her cousin by marriage, Mary S. Ames, was an officer in the Massachusetts Anti-Suffrage Association, and served as vice president of the national anti-suffrage movement.

Blanche was criticized by family members for endangering her marriage and family by publicly expressing her views on women's equality and on birth control.

Her husband, Oakes Ames, the country's leading orchidologist and professor of botany at Harvard University, was a willing collaborator with his wife. He joined her in suffrage rallies throughout the state, endorsed the movement in leading periodicals, marched in pro-suffrage parades and served as chairman of the Men's League for Women's Suffrage.

Theirs was a truly remarkable marriage for the times. It began in 1900, a year after her graduation from Smith College. They collaborated not only in politics, but in botany, publishing, and their love for the environment.

Blanche drew hundreds of analytical sketches of new species of orchards for her husband's seven-volume series, *Orchidaceae: Illustrations and Studies of the Family Orchidaceae*.

A feminist long before it was reasonably fashionable, Oakes at one time decided not to give his bride a wedding ring since he felt it was an archaic sign of marital bondage.

"We are forming a contract. We have an equal voice," Oakes told her shortly before their wedding.

Instead, Blanche's mother gave her the wedding ring that had belonged to her grandmother, Sarah (Hildreth) Butler, a popular Shakespearian actress. Oakes, at the urging of his family, recanted and gave his new bride a wedding ring. For the rest of her life, Blanche Ames wore two wedding bands on her finger.

Family relationships became embittered as Blanche, her husband Oakes and Anna Ames (the widow of Governor Oliver Ames) took on the cause of women's rights against the wishes of the rest of the Ames family.

The defeat of Weeks was not the first time Blanche Ames took on a leading politician over the issue of equality for women. She had no qualms about taking on even the President of the United States, William Howard Taft (1857–1930).

Her pro-suffrage political cartoons appeared in many national magazines and newspapers.

Taft denounced one of Blanche's cartoons in a *Saturday Evening Post* article, calling her work, "unjust and absurd."

No wallflower, she quickly responded with yet another political cartoon called "Our Answer to Mr. Taft."

Politicians weren't the only ones to feel her wrath.

She once accused Charles W. Eliot, President of Harvard University, of being a "victim of arrested development," when he refused to back the suffrage movement.

Blanche Ames was without a doubt a force to be reckoned with, during a period in American History when most well-bred women of her stature were viewed primarily as the ornamental icing on the institutional cake of marriage.

What most people, from Senate hopefuls and U.S. presidents, to even members of her own family, didn't reckon on was her single-minded belief in self-determination for women, not only in politics, but in every aspect of their lives.

She co-founded the Birth Control League of Massachusetts in 1916 as an affiliate group of Margaret Sanger's national effort to educate women on birth control practices.

Besides being a leading proponent of women's right to vote and birth control, she was an artist, illustrator, author and inventor.

Her self-determination carried over into all aspects of her life.

"For her to have an idea was to act, no matter how difficult or impossible," her daughter, Pauline Ames Plimpton, wrote about her. Pauline was the mother of editor and author George Plimpton.

As an artist, she left behind an extensive body of portrait paintings, including many reproductions of the masters that she studied at the Boston Museum of Fine Arts.

She and her brother, Adelbert Ames, Jr., developed what might be considered the first "paint by numbers," color chart system. It was made up of over 4,000 different colors, each numerically coded to correlate to 4,000 different tubes of oil paint.

Using the chart, she was able to create near exact color matches for her reproductions, original paintings and sketches.

By placing one of the color chips against an original painting or matching it to a still-life she was sketching, she could accurately match the color schemes with the corresponding color code she and her brother had devised. Many of her sketches were marked numerically, indicating the color to be used in the final painting.

One of her most famous paintings, an elm tree, hangs in what was once Pauline's room at the family estate in Easton, Massachusetts. At first glance, the painting appears to be a photograph, and only after careful examination can it be determined that it is an amazing life-like painting.

The color chart, along with a host her paintings, remain on display at Borderland, the Ames family estate. The three-story, twenty-room stone mansion, designed by Blanche, was built in 1910 and sits on 1,570 acres of land.

The estate is now managed by the Massachusetts Department of Environmental Management. The property was acquired by the Commonwealth of Massachusetts in 1971, two years after the death of Blanche.

Many of the rooms at Borderland remain furnished as they were when Blanche, Oakes, and their four children lived there. Along with many of Blanche's paintings that hang there, Borderland houses the Ames library, whose 8,000 books were given to the State for safekeeping.

Born in Lowell, Massachusetts, in 1878, Blanche was one of six children born to Adelbert and Blanche (Butler) Ames.

Her father, a native of Maine, was a much-decorated general in the Civil War. He later served as a U.S. Senator and Governor of Mississippi during Reconstruction.

When John F. Kennedy referred to her father as a carpetbagger in his book, *Profiles In Courage*, an incensed Blanche Ames, at the age of eighty, wrote a book refuting the soon-to-be president's assertions. Her book, *Adelbert Ames: Broken Oaths and Reconstruction in Mississippi, 1835–1933*, was published in 1964.

Her family owned woolen mills in Lowell and held financial interests in flour mills in Minnesota. Blanche attended Smith College, where she excelled in art, played rigorous sports, including tennis, and was elected class president in 1899.

She delivered the commencement address at her graduation, where seated in the audience was President William McKinley (1843–1901). In the speech she told the audience that a new age of self-determination was dawning on America. It was the first time, but not the last, that she lectured a United States president on women's rights.

Following their marriage in 1900, Blanche and Oakes Ames moved to Easton, Massachusetts, where they lived with Oakes' mother, Anna. His family had made their fortune from the Ames Shovel Works Company, located in North Easton. The company developed the first lightweight but durable shovel used almost exclusively during the Gold Rush of 1849 and during the Civil War. The Ames family also ran the Union Pacific Railroad.

Blanche and Oakes soon began acquiring farmland in Easton that would later become their Borderland estate. From 1901 to 1910, Blanche had four children: Pauline (1901), Oliver (1903), Amyas (1906), and Evelyn (1910).

Construction on the Blanche-designed stone mansion began in 1910 and was finished a year later. Both Blanche and Oakes were dedicated to preserving the natural beauty of the land. They repaired and expanded dams on the property, developed hiking trails, cleared fields, gardened, and years later, devoted the property to protecting wildlife.

Following passage of the suffrage amendment in 1920, Blanche devoted much of her time and energy to the issue of birth control, engaging in spirited debates with leaders of the Roman Catholic Church over the issue.

In 1941 she became a board member of the New England Hospital for Women and Children, where women could receive medical care from female physicians and nurses. It was not until 1952 that the hospital, faced with mounting financial woes, admitted male doctors to practice.

Along with her political activities, Blanche worked on a variety of inventions, and applied for patents on several of them. Among them were an anti-pollution toilet, a log cutter and a propeller snare for catching low-flying enemy aircraft during World War II. Although Pentagon officials came to Borderland to view the propeller snare device she invented, the war ended shortly after the demonstration, so it was never used.

Oakes Ames died in 1950. Blanche survived him by nineteen years. She passed away at Borderland in 1969 at the age of ninety-one, leaving behind a rich legacy in art and politics—but perhaps more importantly, the legacy of a self-determined life.

Suggested Reading

Ames, Oakes. *A Memoir* (1979).
Harris, Ann. *Women Artists 1550–1950* (1976).
May, Antoinette. *Different Drummers* (1976).
Mitchell, Juliet. *Women's Estate* (1972).
Parker, Elsie. *Growing Up at Sheep's Pasture* (1976).

EPILOGUE
Bridget smiling

Bridget is not one of the many characters in this book. She might be a character in somebody else's book. Good for her. She is quite a character. I will get to Bridget, by and by.

There are, of course, far more New England women who made a difference than the mere fifteen I have included in this book, and their stories should be told.

Perhaps, more importantly, there are many more women from throughout the various regions of the country whose stories should be told. They too made a difference.

If there is one thing that stands out throughout the lives of the fifteen women in this book, it is, I think, their overriding courage and determination, despite great odds, to do what they felt was right.

That is important. It was important then and it is important now.

In doing what was right, in whatever historical period they existed, the women in this book have taught us all several important lessons.

The first is that established institutions are the last place to look to for significant reforms in our society. Throughout history, contemporary thought, culture and even writing has not supported many of the significant social changes.

The bastions of church, state, business and popular culture are far too entrenched in the *status quo* to ever conceive of, or substantially support, needed changes in our culture.

The second lesson I believe these women have taught us is that whenever anyone, woman or man, speaks out on an issue, they will be labeled a "radical."

Throughout American history, some people think they can make an undesirable issue disappear by branding the person advocating change a "radical." All change is radical. Conversely, all radical change ultimately becomes the norm.

It was "radical" for Abigail Adams to ask her husband to give women in America the same rights as men, following the American Revolution. And, by society's standards at the time, it was radical for Dorothea Dix to speak out on behalf of reforming standards of care for the mentally ill in the country. It was even at one time considered radical for women in America to vote.

How foolish we have all been.

The last thing that I think the fifteen women in this book have taught us is that it is important to listen to your heart. It is the message that truly matters. The women in this book changed things and our world not because they listened to the so-called experts or authorities. They listened to their hearts.

Knowing what is right is not a matter of whether you are liberal or conservative, Republican or Democrat. No one has cornered the market on what is right, not even religions.

Someday, some future society will look back and think how ignorant it was for the Catholic Church to ban women from being priests. And how cosmically stupid those who banned it were. History is a brutal teacher.

There are many changes in our society that we take for granted now. Think of how absurd the notions were that women could not serve in the military, or that no woman should be a Supreme Court Justice, or that young girls could not play organized sports.

The notion that these few simple things were once rabidly protested against at some stage of their development seems alien to us, but someone, somewhere had to take that first giant step, despite the institutions that aligned themselves against them, despite being labeled "radical" and despite all the cultural norms.

Perhaps one of the most serious illusions that we have been lulled into believing is that all the important issues have somehow been miraculously resolved. They haven't.

There so many issues in our society that need to be addressed and so many more in the future that will need to be. Many of these issues will resolved, I believe, by women.

That is why I believe it is important for all parents to tell their daughters that there were many women who helped change our culture and society for the good, whatever the odds stacked against them.

Tell them this: It will not be easy. Do not look to existing institutions for support. There is nothing wrong with being labeled as a radical.

And tell them: Listen to your heart—listen to what you instinctively know is true and right and good.

One last thing: Tell them not to be afraid. We love them. And we're counting on them, all of them.

All this brings me back to Bridget smiling.

Somehow, when we are children, it seems so much easier to listen to our hearts, to know, instinctively, what is going on all around us, to read the subtle signals of the cosmos.

That is what Bridget smiling is all about.

Bridget is my niece.

Many years ago she used to live in the house next door to me.

Back then, she and my son, Nathan, were about the same age, five or six years old.

They were inseparable and used to play together all the time. Often, Nathan would go next door to my sister's house to play with Bridget.

One day, Nathan was sitting by one of the windows facing onto Bridget's house, staring out.

"What's the matter?" I asked. "Why don't you go next door to Bridget's?"

"She's not home," he said. And then, completely out of the blue, he said, "Dad, can we go to Lincoln Park today?"

At that time, Lincoln Park was a wonderful old amusement park, complete with a huge ferris wheel, a rickety roller coaster, a faltering merry-go-round and a none-too-scary Fun House.

But none of this mattered to Nathan. We had taken him and Bridget there many times and it always filled them both with the most obvious joy.

Lincoln Park has since been torn down. Ironically, I miss its forlorn demeanor—its bustling, crowded arcade of parents and children holding hands, its greasy midway, filled with odd-looking carney folks, its creaky, faulty amusement rides, the criers hawking fixed ring-toss games, and its stale scent of popcorn, hot dogs and cotton candy.

Amusement parks like Lincoln Park have vanished from the face of our American landscape, willy-nilly, making room for the taciturn, sterile likes of Disney World. Too bad. I am not amused by the mendacity of places like Disney World.

There was always something uniquely compelling about the old amusement parks. Maybe, somebody, somewhere decided there was too much amusement in the world already. Perhaps they thought, we all should keep our minds

EPILOGUE: BRIDGET SMILING

on business and forget about amusing ourselves any more than we have to. Who knows?

In any event, back so many years ago, when amusement parks still populated the world, Nathan asked me, out of the blue, if we could go to Lincoln Park.

"Why do you want to go to Lincoln Park?" I asked him.

"Because Bridget is going to Lincoln Park," he said forlornly.

"How do you know Bridget is going to Lincoln Park?" I asked. "Her mother didn't say anything to me. Did you talk to her?"

"No," Nathan informed me. "But I saw her in the car with her mother backing out of the driveway," he said.

"Oh, well, maybe she was going to the store. She could have been going anywhere," I explained to him.

"Nope. She's going to Lincoln Park," he said.

"How do you know that?" I asked.

"Because I saw her in the back seat and Bridget was smiling," he said.

A dead giveaway.

As we grow older, we seem to lose that youthful, hopeful intuition about life. Too bad.

With the passage of time we seem to become deaf mutes when it comes to listening to what our heart tells us.

I hope that this book becomes for everyone that reads it what Bridget's smile was for my young son, Nathan—a cosmic signal from the heart that something wonderfully adventurous is happening and that we want to be part of it.

I can tell you this, whenever I see someone smiling for no apparent reason, I find myself saying, "They must be going to Lincoln Park."

ABOUT THE AUTHOR

J. North Conway is the author of four books, including *New England Women of Substance: Fifteen Who Made a Difference; American Literacy: Fifty Books That Define Our Culture and Ourselves; From Coup To Nuts: A Revolutionary Cookbook* and the poetry book, *One Horse Universe*. He is a former Boston University professor and lives in Taunton, Massachusetts.

LOOK FOR THESE OTHER FINE BOOKS FROM COVERED BRIDGE PRESS AND DOUGLAS CHARLES PRESS

Yankee Cinderella	Thomas B. Smith	$12.95
Until I Have No Country: A Novel of King Philip's War in New England	Michael Tougias	$12.95
New England's Most Intriguing Gangsters, Rascals, Rogues and Thieves	Marc Songini	$12.95
New England Ghost Files Charles T. Robinson		$14.95
New England Ghost Files (cassette) Charles Turek Robinson, read by Joseph Citro		$9.95
Native New England: The Long Journey Charles Turek Robinson		$16.95
The Sparrowhawk Curse	Robin Moore	$12.95
The Boston Bogeyman: And More New England Mysteries Curt Norris		$10.95
The Man Who Talked to Trees … and More Strange New England Tales	Curt Norris	$12.95
New England's Most Sensational Murders Marc Songini		$10.95

New England Town Affairs Charles J. Lincoln		$12.95
Visions: Cape Cod and The Vineyard Harold Wilson		$9.95
Magnificent Mainers	Jeff Hollingsworth	$14.95
Don Bosquet's Rhode Island Cookbook Sara Clark, ed.		$10.95
The Lobster Lover's Cookbook, Revised Edition Brian M. Coffey		$9.95
Old Sturbridge Village Calendar		$7.95
The Boston Dictionary	John Powers	$10.95
New England's Best Family Getaways Dan and Roberta LaPlante		$14.95
Yankee Wildlife	Hilbert R. Siegler	$12.95

Please ask for these titles at your local bookstore first.

To order direct, send a check for the price of the book(s) plus $3.00 shipping and handling for the first book and $.50 for each additional book to:

Covered Bridge Press
440 Mendon Road
North Attleboro, MA 02760

Thank you for your patronage of
New England's Own Publisher!